Planning it safe:

How to Control Liability and Risk in Volunteer Programs

**Concrete Suggestions,
Clear Definitions, and a
Preventive Approach
to Managing Legal Risk and Liability**

Project Co-sponsored by

Minnesota Office of Citizenship and Volunteer Services, Department of Administration

Minnesota Department of Human Services

Minnesota State Bar Association

Guidebook published by

Minnesota Office of Citizenship and Volunteer Services

Minnesota Department of Administration

117 University Avenue, St. Paul, Minnesota 55155

February 1992, April 1998

Minnesota Office of Citizenship and Volunteer Services, Department of Administration

Minnesota Department of Human Services

U.S. Department of Health and Human Services

GRANT NO. 1-9101-MN-1400

All rights reserved.

Printed in the United States of America.

Library of Congress Catalog Card Number 92-80708

ISBN 1-881282-00-7

Contents

Quick Reference Guide (back cover)

Acknowledgments

Foreword

Acknowledgments

We would like to thank the many people who contributed to this edition and the original publication.

Staff Managers

Laura Lee Geraghty and Charley Ravine, contractor
   Minnesota Office of Citizenship and Volunteer Services, Minnesota Department of Administration
Mike Newman and Melissa Eystad
   Community and Human Resource Development, Minnesota Department of Human Services
Lisa Wilde
   Minnesota State Bar Association
Bonnie Esposito and Charley Ravine, Contractor (Second Edition)
   Minnesota Office of Citizenship and Volunteer Services, Minnesota Department of Administration

Original Task Force Members

Valerie Holmgren, Chair ....Minnesota Office of Citizenship and Volunteer Services Advisory Committee
Donna Allan..Office of Transit, Minnesota Department of Transportation
Steve Brand..Robins, Kaplan, Miller & Ciresi and Minnesota State Bar Association
David Cumming ....Minnesota Insurance Information Center, and Minnesota Office of Citizenship and
                                                             Volunteer Services Advisory Committee
John Dooley ....Minnesota Association of Townships
Lisa Engebretson.................................Sexual Offenses Services (SOS) of Ramsey County
Melissa Eystad ....Community and Human Resource Development,
                                                             Minnesota Department of Human Services
Laura Lee Geraghty.............................Minnesota Office of Citizenship and Volunteer Services,
                                                             Minnesota Department of Administration
Barb Gustafson ....National Retiree Volunteer Center
John Harris ....Faegre & Benson, and Minnesota State Bar Association
Shelley Jacobson ....Chrysalis, A Center for Women
Fred Johnson.......................................Risk Management Division, Minnesota Department of Administration
Kate Jowett...Minnesota Association of Volunteer Centers, and
                                                             Voluntary Action Center of the St. Paul Area, Inc.
Byron Laher ....United Way of Greater Minneapolis
Jeff Lang ....Parker, Satrom, O'Neil, Lindberg & McKinnis, P.A.
Debra Ledvina ....Community Volunteer
Bob Mitchell ....Big Brothers|Big Sisters
H. Camilla Nelson ....Charities Division, Minnesota Attorney General's Office
Pat Plunkett...Moore, Costello & Hart, and Minnesota State Bar Association
Kathy Pontius ....Minnesota Senate Counsel and Research
Charley Ravine ....Management Assistance Program (MAP)
Beverly Robinson ....Minnesota Association of Volunteer Directors, and
                                                             Minnesota Masonic Home Care Center
Jean Roessler ....Minnesota Council of Directors of Health Care Volunteers, and
                                                             Fairview Ridges Hospital

Kevin J. Rupp ....Ratwik, Roszak, Bergstrom, Maloney & Bartel, P.A., and

Minnesota State Bar Association

Bob Sonnee...Volunteer, Retired Risk Manager

Joanne Whiterabbit ....Corporate Volunteerism Council and Cray Research

Karen Zupancich ....Health Care Auxiliary of Minnesota

Editor

Margret Alnes ....Editor (Volunteer through the Management Assistance Program for Nonprofits)

Graphic Design

Siu Lee ....Graphic Designer, Minnegasco, Inc.

(Volunteer through the Management Assistance Program for Nonprofits)

Legal Issues Researchers/Writers

John Herbert.......................................Minnesota Office of Citizenship and Volunteer Services Volunteer

Kellie Nealon ....Dorsey & Whitney

Risk Management Researcher/Writer

Bob Sonnee...Volunteer, Retired Risk Manager

Student Intern

Jane Lewis ....Metropolitan State University

Advisors and Reviewers

Paula Beugen ....Minnesota Office of Citizenship and Volunteer Services,

Minnesota Department of Administration

Thomas Campbell ....Adult Protection, Minnesota Department of Human Services

Don Gemberling ....Data Protection Division, Minnesota Department of Administration

Kenneth Mentz ....Appeals and Contracts, Minnesota Department of Human Services

Joan Monahan ....Child Protection, Minnesota Department of Human Services

Mike Newman ....Community and Human Resource Development,

Minnesota Department of Human Services

Joseph Piwoschuk ....Personnel, Minnesota Department of Human Services

Lisa Wilde..Minnesota State Bar Association

Fred Johnson......................................Minnesota Department of Administration, Director Risk Management

Foreword

Second Edition Note:

*Welcome to the second edition of **Planning it Safe: How to Control Liability and Risk in Volunteer Programs.** Since the first printing in 1992, 4,000 copies of this guidebook have been produced for volunteer and risk management professionals throughout the country. Many changes have taken place in the law since 1992, and this second edition updates the entire liability section of this book.*

The mission of the Minnesota Office of Citizenship and Volunteer Services (MOCVS), a division of the state Department of Administration, is to promote citizen participation efforts, increase the impact of volunteer programs, and stimulate public/private partnerships in Minnesota. In this role, MOCVS is called upon to identify emerging trends and address concerns in the field of volunteerism. The Minnesota Department of Human Services (MDHS), provides volunteer programs in the human services system statewide. In the late 1980s, both agencies experienced a dramatic increase in the number and complexity of questions relating to legal issues affecting volunteers and volunteer programs. The issues covered a range of topics, including professional liability, data privacy, abusive relationships, and human rights. It was apparent that there was a need at that time for materials that would assist volunteer leaders in addressing some of these basic concerns.

In response, the two agencies felt the development of a guidebook explaining legal concerns of volunteer programs would begin to address the need for information in this area, and decided to collaborate on the project. MOCVS provided the leadership, staff direction, and coordination, while MDHS provided funding and technical assistance.

Because the involvement of the legal community was instrumental to the success of the effort, the Minnesota State Bar Association was also involved and became a project cosponsor and provided several attorneys to assist in the effort.

In the fall of 1990 a task force was convened to provide direction in the development of a legal issues guidebook. The 30-member task force was chaired by a member of the MOCVS Advisory Committee and included representatives from the fields of volunteer administration, law, insurance, and risk management, as well as policy makers from business, voluntary organizations, and local units of government. This guidebook is the result of the leadership, hard work and dedication of the task force members and other volunteers who contributed ideas, skills, and time.

From the first meeting it was obvious that the vision of the members, coupled with the needs of the volunteer community, would lead us beyond the original concept of a short, simple guidebook delineating current laws that impact volunteers and volunteer programs. Among the conclusions of the task force were that:

- There was a great need for guidance in determining and managing risks associated with volunteers and volunteer programs.

- This guidebook could only provide a first step toward meeting the needs for better information on legal concerns and risk management. More in-depth research and materials needed to be developed on specific topics.

- There was a need to develop and deliver risk management training for volunteer program leaders to supplement the information in the guidebook.

- The guidebook must encourage consistent movement toward better, safer volunteer management practices without setting such high expectations that many smaller volunteer programs could not continue to function.

- There was a need to allay fears, correct misinformation, and educate the public and potential volunteers as to why volunteer programs sometimes need to screen volunteers more carefully today.

- Board members, executive directors, and risk managers in agencies, as well as representatives from the legal and insurance fields, could benefit from clarification of volunteer-related laws and guidance on risk management techniques.

In using this guidebook there are several things to keep in mind. First, in order to keep the guidebook readable and appropriate for a broad audience, we limited the content to those areas affecting large numbers of volunteer programs. It is not intended to answer all questions that might arise.

Secondly, ***this guidebook is not designed to provide legal advice.*** It aims to provide basic information and background on laws and risk management for policy makers and volunteer leaders. Specific questions and concerns should be directed to your legal counsel.

Finally, the guidebook is not intended to provide "hard and fast" rules for working with volunteers. While it will provide guidance, common sense and thoughtful management should prevail in this rapidly changing area.

This guidebook was the first step to address the need for both a better understanding of laws affecting volunteer programs and techniques for managing risks. Since its publication the project co-sponsors and other organizations have continued to address challenges as we strive to strengthen our volunteer programs. The project co-sponsors and other organizations are addressing these challenges in a number of ways:

- The Minnesota Office of Citizenship and Volunteer Services provides training in risk management for volunteer programs.

- The Minnesota Office of Citizenship and Volunteer Services and the Minnesota Department of Transportation developed *Getting There Safely - Insurance & Liability Information for Volunteer Drivers.* This brochure is designed specific to the concerns of volunteer transportation programs.

- Several Minnesota organizations have collaborated to produce *Legal-Ease,* a quarterly newsletter for nonprofit managers and boards, through which emerging legal concerns can be addressed. These organizations include the Management Assistance Project, Minnesota Council of Nonprofits, Minnesota Office of Citizenship and Volunteer Services, the Center for Nonprofit Management-University of St. Thomas, Resources and Counseling for the Arts, and the United Way.

We hope you find this guidebook helpful. The Minnesota Office of Citizenship and Volunteer Services welcomes comments and suggestions as it continues to develop new resources that will ensure the effective and rewarding involvement of volunteers in problem solving and service delivery to meet community needs.

Bonnie Esposito, Director
Minnesota Office of Citizenship and Volunteer Services
Department of Administration

Introduction

What this guidebook is about

Does your organization involve volunteers? If so, you've no doubt discovered the advantages of doing so. The benefits of a volunteer program can be great, and those benefits have been well documented.

At the same time, legal risks are associated with operating any program, including a volunteer program. Your organization might become liable for wrongs committed by a member or volunteer. Examples are as diverse as the organizations that involve volunteers. A Meals-On-Wheels driver runs personal errands while delivering the food; in the process, the food spoils. A Girl Scout leader takes her group on a field trip, and during that trip one of the girls is injured. Volunteers for an advocacy group take part in a demonstration; and in the heat of the protest, one of them throws a rock through a window.

Situations like these raise the issue of liability: Who is legally responsible for such acts? This question is well worth considering before a loss or lawsuit occurs. More specifically:

- Can a volunteer's acts make your organization liable if another person is harmed?
- Is your volunteer protected by law from any liability, or can the volunteer be held liable for certain actions?
- If held personally liable, will the volunteer be defended or protected against financial loss?
- How can managing our risks and losses help us protect the people we serve?

The purpose of this guidebook is to help you answer questions like these. It is not meant to "scare" anyone or to raise fears of lawsuit. Rather, it is a guide for volunteer programs, organizations, and individual volunteers concerning their legal rights and responsibilities in performing volunteer services. Ultimately, this guidebook can help you better protect the people you serve.

Typically, volunteer programs are only one part, though a major part, of an organization. Even so, the issues addressed in this guidebook apply to all aspects of a nonprofit organization.

Note: This guidebook does not give legal advice

This guidebook provides information only. It is not a substitute for legal advice related to the facts and circumstances of an individual volunteer, program, or organization. Also, the laws in this area are constantly changing, so do not consider this information to be the final word. This guidebook aims only to introduce you to the overall issues and to help you begin asking the right questions.

How to use this guidebook

To get the most benefit from this guidebook, read all of it. Issues discussed in one place are often expanded on in other sections.

The guidebook is divided into five parts. All of them relate to the current legal rights and responsibilities of volunteers, volunteer programs, and organizations that involve volunteers. Note that each major section includes a preview and summary.

Part One discusses liability for personal injury.

Part Two speaks to business liability. This includes liability of officers and directors of an organization, and issues that arise from terminating a volunteer.

Part Three explains the possible ways that a volunteer, volunteer program, or organization is protected from liability.

Part Four explains basic concepts in risk management. It answers such questions as: What is risk management? What are effective policies for risk management? And, how do we implement a risk management program? The purpose is to help your organization identify possible risks and treat them. Included are checklists that can help you begin a risk management program.

Part Five explains in more detail some specific risks your organization might face. It also includes some checklists for you to use in developing a risk management program.

One more word about scope: Parts One through Three deal mainly with issues faced by organizations within Minnesota, except where noted otherwise. However, Parts Four and Five, which deal with risk management, have applications across the country. Any organization that involves volunteers, no matter what state it's located in, can benefit from the ideas included here.

The appendices to this guidebook include additional checklists for risk management and a list of recommended materials.

Note that the material in this guidebook is only an introduction to legal issues and risk management. There are many more detailed materials and opportunities for training in these areas. To find out more, see the resources listed beginning on page 82.

Some key terms for you to know

Understanding some key terms will help you get the most out of this guidebook. The following definitions emerge from court cases involving volunteers over the last 20 years.

Volunteers and volunteer programs

For the purposes of this guidebook, a volunteer is someone who chooses to perform services for an organization without compensation.

We can look at volunteers in two different ways. First, there is the "pure" volunteer. Consider the people who stop at the scene of an accident to see if anyone is hurt and to offer help. These people are pure volunteers. That is, they are not acting as directed by an agency or program. This category includes people who help out in an emergency.

Second, there is the gratuitous employee. This is the person we normally think of as a volunteer. The gratuitous employee has a specific role or job description within an organization but does not get paid.

We can also talk about volunteer programs and organizations in three different settings:

- Nonprofit agencies that involve volunteers.
- Community programs that are not incorporated, composed entirely of volunteers.
- A government agency that involves volunteers.

Compensation

Our definition of volunteer mentioned compensation. But what is compensation? In Minnesota, the Nonprofit Corporation Act defines this term as it relates to volunteer directors, officers, and agents of a nonprofit organization. According to this law, compensation is anything of value given to a volunteer, but not reimbursement for expenses. It is not clear whether this definition applies in all situations, but it is a standard from which to start.

What does this definition mean in everyday terms? Some examples can help make this clear. Many nonprofit organizations, for instance, reimburse their board of directors for the expenses of attending a convention. Such occasional reimbursement would probably not be considered compensation.

Suppose, however, that a nonprofit camping organization gives volunteers free use of its premises during the summer. Or, suppose that a food shelf gives each of its volunteers a weekly basket of free groceries. Such gifts could well be considered compensation.

A stipend is an amount paid beyond reimbursement for hard expenses, such as mileage. It appears that a stipend qualifies as compensation. To be sure, check the legislation and regulations that apply to your program.

What this guidebook does not cover

This guidebook does not address volunteer programs in a for-profit corporation. Examples are volunteer programs in for-profit hospitals and corporate volunteer programs. These programs have different concerns, although some of the information in this guidebook may apply to them. (This is particularly true in the area of risk management.)

In addition, another type of liability—criminal liability—is not addressed in this guidebook.

PART ONE

LIABILITY FOR PERSONAL INJURY TO A THIRD PERSON

Part One discusses the following topics:

- It's a fact: Charitable organizations can be sued

- Knowing when your organization or volunteers can be held liable

- Four types of tort liability

- Negligence

- Strict liability

- Intentional misconduct and criminal conduct

- Invasion of privacy

- Special considerations regarding abuse of vulnerable persons

This discussion of legal issues is based on Minnesota law. Please note that statutes and case law can change, and that different states can have different laws on these subjects. However, the general concepts regarding liability may apply beyond Minnesota.

IT'S A FACT: CHARITABLE ORGANIZATIONS CAN BE SUED

First, a word about charitable immunity. You've probably heard people say that a charitable organization cannot be held liable for injuries to another person. This doctrine of charitable immunity does not apply in Minnesota. The state Supreme Court abolished charitable immunity in 1928.[1] Charitable organizations in Minnesota can be sued just as any other organization or corporation. However, certain specific statutes give charitable organizations some special protections. Part Three of this guidebook discusses these.

Other states deal with the issue of charitable immunity in a variety of ways; for example, Iowa, North Dakota, and Wisconsin have also abolished charitable immunity.

KNOWING WHEN YOUR ORGANIZATION OR VOLUNTEERS CAN BE HELD LIABLE

Knowing when your organization or volunteers can be held liable means learning a few legal concepts. It helps to know something about cases where an organization or volunteer can be held liable for injury to a third person. Personal injury falls under tort law. A tort is a wrong that harms an individual. Torts can result from a particular action taken by the volunteer, whether or not it's intentional, or from a failure to act when there is a duty to do so.

But a tort does not include a breach of contract. For example, if another driver runs a stop sign and collides with your car, that person has tort liability. In contrast, if you take a computer to a local office machine store to be fixed, and the store fails to perform the repair. This would be a breach of contract, not a tort.

Suppose that while at work for your organization a volunteer harms another person. That person might sue both the volunteer and the organization for compensation. Most often the injured person will sue; sometimes the parents or guardian of the injured person will bring the suit. This often happens, for example, when the injured person is a child or is incapacitated. In any case, injured persons will want to recover for damages.

A volunteer can be held personally liable for a particular action. And the court might also hold the volunteer's organization liable. One way the organization might be held liable for harm caused by a volunteer is under the legal doctrine of "respondeat superior." Or the organization can be held liable under the theory that it failed to properly select, train or supervise the volunteer.

The doctrine of respondeat superior says that organizations are responsible for the acts of employees acting within the scope of their duties. It also can apply to volunteers who are acting in the scope of their volunteer duties. Respondeat superior originated in the idea that masters have control over their servants. Over the years it has changed to mean that the employer has control over the employee who is acting within the scope of employment.

This concept of control applies as well to organizations that involve volunteers just as it applies to employees. The organization might be held legally liable even if it was not negligent and used due care in selecting, training or supervising volunteers.

Failing to use proper care when selecting, training and supervising volunteers presents another way an organization can be held liable for injuries caused by a volunteer. An organization has certain duties regarding hiring, training and supervising its employees, and these duties are likely to apply to volunteers as well. These duties can create liability for a volunteer's actions, even if those actions are outside the scope of the volunteer's duties. For example, intentional injuries (such as molesting a child) are clearly not within the scope of any volunteer's duty. But an organization might be liable for those intentional injuries if the organization had not taken the appropriate steps when selecting or supervising its volunteers.

In light of these trends, it is essential for your organization to take good faith steps and follow general personnel practices when working with volunteers. For example, job descriptions should define the scope of the volunteer's duties and supervision. In addition, orientation sessions and performance reviews can inform volunteers of standards of conduct and their exposure to safety risks. For more detail, see Parts Four and Five of this guidebook.

A recent Massachusetts case demonstrates one way a charitable organization can be found liable for injuries.[2] In this case, a Catholic high school held a dance to raise money for the student council. There had been fights at previous dances, so the high school arranged for several chaperons and a uniformed police officer to attend the dance. But a serious fight broke out and several students were injured, including a boy who was stabbed. A jury found the school was negligent in supervising the dance and awarded damages for the student's injuries. The appellate court upheld the jury's verdict. The student presented expert testimony that the precautions were not sufficient to prevent injuries to students. The expert pointed out that three or four chaperons with no training or plan were not enough to stop fights. The expert also explained that the school should have stopped the dance immediately when the uniformed police officer failed to arrive at the beginning of the dance. And the expert noted that the lighting was too dim and no one was checking identification to make sure all those who attended were high school students. All of these factors convinced the jury that the school was negligent.

FOUR TYPES OF TORT LIABILITY

Under tort law, there are four types of liability that concern volunteers and volunteer organizations:

- Negligence
- Strict liability
- Intentional misconduct and criminal conduct
- Invasion of privacy rights

We will discuss each of these areas in turn.

Negligence

Four factors establish negligence:

- A duty of care to the person harmed
- A breach of that duty
- Direct or proximate cause
- An actual harm to the third person (damages)

The courts will consider these factors when deciding whether negligence occurred. Each factor deserves a more complete explanation.

Duty of care to the person harmed

Before volunteers or organizations can be held responsible for negligence, they must owe a duty of care to the injured person. If there is no duty, there is no legal responsibility. Usually the volunteer and volunteer organization do owe a duty of care to the people they serve.

Whether or not a duty exists depends on the specific facts of the situation. Usually, courts apply what is called the "reasonable person" standard. This refers to what a reasonable, prudent person would do under the same circumstances to avoid a foreseeable injury.

Suppose, for example, that volunteers who work in a congregate dining hall do not prepare food carefully. As a result, the people who eat there get sick. What is the duty of care? Reasonable, prudent people would wash their hands before preparing the food. They would also keep the work area clean to avoid spreading germs, which is a foreseeable risk. In this example, then, the volunteers have a duty to wash their hands and keep their work area clean.

The "reasonable person" standard is an objective standard; that is, it may be different than what an individual volunteer or organization considers reasonable. For instance, hospital volunteers without medical training may judge it reasonable to not personally intervene if they see a patient choking. Yet it is reasonable for these volunteers to go for emergency help anyway. The volunteers could be held liable for not seeking assistance.

Besides being an objective standard, the "reasonable person" standard is an adult standard. In other words, it is based on what a reasonable adult would do in the given situation. However, there are three exceptions to this standard. They apply to children, professionals, and standards set by statute.

- Children will generally be held to a lesser standard of care than adults. The standard for children is measured by what a child of the same age, experience, and intelligence would do in the same circumstances.[3] However, this lower standard of care does not apply when children participate in adult activities, such as driving a car or boat.[4] This poses specific concerns for the organization that involves children as volunteers. Among them are the type of training offered, the age and prior experience of the child, and the nature of the volunteer task. Case law in Minnesota says that this standard also applies to people with mental disabilities.[5]

- In some circumstances, then, a child might not be held liable for injury. Even so, the organization could be held liable if, for instance, the volunteer task was beyond the child's capability or experience. Assigning a task that is clearly beyond a person's capability is called negligent entrustment. How do you determine what activities are appropriate for children? Be sure to review OSHA regulations and laws for child labor.

- Volunteers who are professionals, such as doctors, nurses, lawyers, or accountants, are held to the standard of care for that particular profession. The profession itself usually sets that standard. Generally, this means acting with the same degree of care and skill that other members of the profession would exercise in similar circumstances.[6] This standard applies whether the professional is paid or unpaid.

- Standards of care can be set by statute—that is, defined by law. However, violating the statute won't automatically impose liability on a volunteer or organization. Injured persons still need to show that they are protected under the statute, and that the statute intends to prevent the kind of harm they experienced.[7] The kind of negligence involved here is known as "negligence per se". This means that the law defines the duty of care and how that duty is breached.

Some specific examples of duties that exist:

Good Samaritan Laws These laws generally require a person to help someone who is seriously hurt in an emergency. Minnesota's Good Samaritan Law establishes a duty to help out in an emergency:

> A person at the scene of an emergency who knows that another person is exposed to or has suffered grave physical harm, shall, to the extent that the person can do so without danger or peril to self or others, give reasonable assistance to the exposed person. Reasonable assistance may include obtaining or attempting to obtain aid from law enforcement or medical personnel.[8]

Working With Children In Minnesota, the general standard of care is higher for people who work with children.[9] This means that working with children calls for greater care than working with adults. For example, an organization staffed with teenage volunteers for a highway clean-up project would need more adult supervisors than a similar outing with adult volunteers.

Selecting, Training and Supervising Volunteers Organizations have duties of care when selecting, training and supervising employees. These same duties probably apply to volunteers as well. This type of claim usually comes up when the employee or volunteer is acting beyond the scope of his or her duties. This duty is discussed in more detail later in Part One, under "Intentional misconduct and criminal conduct."

When No Duty of Care Exists Even where a duty of care does not exist, the volunteer or organization must act carefully. In short, if you decide to help someone, you must act in a way that does not make matters worse.

Consider, for example, a parent who volunteers in an elementary school. This parent encounters a child who is injured on the playground and needs cardiopulmonary resuscitation (CPR). If the parent undertakes CPR without knowing how, this action could well make matters worse. Suppose, instead, that the parent decides to get someone who knows CPR; this action is consistent with the duty of care.

Breach of duty

Once a duty of care is established, the issue is whether the volunteer or organization failed to meet that standard of care. Deciding the specific duty is usually more involved than deciding whether the person breached that duty. Take the dining hall example from the discussion above. A volunteer serving food has a duty to wash his hands and clean up his work area. If the volunteer does not wash his hands, he has breached his duty of care.

Direct or proximate cause

Causation is the next element in a tort claim. This simply means that there must be a link between the breach of duty and the injury suffered by the plaintiff. Sometimes, the negligence directly causes an injury, for instance, when a volunteer leaves a wet spot on the floor that causes someone to fall. Other times, the injury is not the direct result of the negligence; yet the negligence made it possible for the injury to happen.

To understand this, think in terms of an unbroken chain of events leading from the negligent act to the injury. Suppose that a supervisor asks a volunteer to mop the floor immediately. Yet the supervisor does this during a time when the floor will be heavily used. Further, the supervisor does not tell the volunteer to rope off the wet area, or to post any "Caution: Wet Floor" signs. Here the supervisor's negligence causes the injury.

Actual harm to a third party (damages)

The requirement of actual harm simply means that there must be some compensable injury involved– an injury for which a court can award damages. Damages can include medical bills, lost wages, the long-term cost of physical injuries, property damage, and the like.

The following chart summarizes our discussion of negligence issues as they relate to volunteers and volunteer organizations.

SUMMARY OF LIABILITY FOR NEGLIGENCE

Pure Volunteer

If the volunteer is injured, then. . . .

The volunteer must show more than ordinary negligence to recover damages for an injury. Any volunteer assumes a minimum risk of injury.

Even though the pure volunteer's acts benefit a person or organization, these acts are unexpected. The pure volunteer cannot use them as a basis to recover damages.

If the volunteer injures another, then . . . .

The injured person must show more than ordinary negligence to recover for damages.

Good Samaritan Laws hold that it is fine to offer help, and is actually required in some situations, but there are limits to what the pure volunteer can legally do. The person must be responsible for actions beyond ordinary negligence.

Gratuitous Employee

If the volunteer is injured, then . . .

As with a pure volunteer, this person must show more than ordinary negligence to recover damages.

This idea is grounded in laws about employees. Gratuitous employees are responsible for actions and activities under their control. They also have a duty to look for and react to danger—for example, when climbing on a ladder that is already broken or unstable.

If a volunteer injures another, then . . .

The injured person must go through a series of steps to recover for damages from the organization.

First, a court will look at whether the volunteer's negligence caused the injury:
• Was a duty of care owed to the injured person?
• Was there a breach in that duty of care?
• Was the action or inaction of the volunteer the cause of the injury?
• Was there actual injury or harm to the individual?

Under the doctrine of respondeat superior (the employer is responsible for the acts of the employee), the organization might be liable if the injured person can show:

1. Was there an employer/employee-like relationship between the organization and the volunteer? Did the "employer" (volunteer organization) have some degree of direction and control over the activities of the volunteer? If so, both the organization and volunteer could be held liable.

2. Was the activity within the volunteer's scope of the duties?

The organization can also be liable if the activity was outside the scope of the volunteer's duties. Here, a court will look at whether the organization was negligent in selecting, training or supervising the volunteer.

Strict liability

Strict liability refers to liability that is imposed whether or not there was negligence. Typically this standard is established by statute. For example, workers' compensation is a form of strict liability. According to law, the employer is liable for injury to an employee even if the employee was negligent.

Another example is the duty of professionals to report suspected sexual abuse of a child or vulnerable adult. Here liability is imposed by statute.

Sometimes strict liability occurs even where no statute applies. This can happen with hazardous or unusual activities, such as use of explosives, flammable material, or wild animals. Volunteers are not often involved in such activities (although we might find a volunteer helping with a fireworks display). If an injury results from hazardous activity, a court might apply strict liability. This could be true even if no negligence took place.

Intentional misconduct and criminal conduct

If a volunteer intentionally injures someone or commits a criminal act, the volunteer will be responsible for any harm caused. This is the case, for example, if a volunteer intentionally hits someone or assaults someone with a weapon. The organization can be held liable under the doctrine of respondeat superior or for failing to properly select, train or supervise its volunteers.

When there is intentional misconduct, the acts are usually seen as beyond the scope of the volunteer's duties so the organization is not liable under the doctrine of respondeat superior, which was discussed in the section on "Negligence" above.

This is not always true, however. Some intentional actions could fall within the volunteer's duties. Suppose, for example, that a nonprofit organization "hires" a volunteer off-duty police officer to provide security at a gathering where liquor is served. Someone begins a fist fight, and the officer decides to escort that person out of the room. In the process, the officer breaks the person's arm. The police officer is sued. If the court decides that the officer actions fell within the scope of volunteer duties, then the nonprofit organization could be held liable.

In Minnesota, injured persons can sue organizations for an employee's intentional actions that are outside the scope of the employee's duties if the organization was negligent in hiring, retaining, training or supervising the employee. The same legal concepts likely apply to volunteers as well as employees.

Negligent hiring occurs when an organization "hires" someone when the organization actually knows the person has a history of violence.[10] It can also occur when the organization would have been able to learn about the person's violent tendencies with a "reasonable investigation." For example, suppose an organization knew a person had a recent history of sexual abuse and had just been released from prison. It would be negligent to hire the person in a job that involved supervising children.

Organizations are generally not required to do a criminal background check on a volunteer unless specifically required by a regulation, as discussed in the later section "When background checks are required for volunteers."

Negligent retention occurs when an organization learns about problems with an employee after hiring the person, and fails to take sufficient precautions to protect others.[11] For example, an organization may not know about a person's criminal record at the beginning, but may learn about it later. Once the organization knows that a person has a tendency to be violent, then the organization must do what is necessary to protect others. This may mean reassigning the person to different duties.

Negligent training occurs when an organization assigns a job to someone, but then fails to give that person appropriate training to perform the functions of that job. For example, suppose an organization assigned someone to operate a piece of equipment at a construction site. The organization would be negligent if it did not provide proper training on how to operate the equipment.

Negligent supervision occurs when an organization fails to use ordinary care to supervise its employees.[12] Here, an organization must consider what harm is foreseeable, and take the necessary steps to supervise the employee so the harm does not occur.

Although these concepts come up in the employment area, it is likely that they would also apply to the selection, retention, training and supervision of volunteers.

SPECIAL CONSIDERATIONS REGARDING ABUSE AND NEGLECT OF VULNERABLE PERSONS

Minnesota law makes a special requirement of any professional in contact with children or vulnerable adults. The term children refers to minors--persons under age 18. Vulnerable adults are those who--because of mental, physical, or emotional impairment--are unable or unlikely to report abuse or neglect.

Professionals must report to county authorities if they have reason to believe a child or vulnerable adult has been abused or neglected.[13] The law imposes a criminal penalty for those who are required to report but fail to do so. Identities of persons making reports are strictly protected by statute.

The actual wording of the law makes clear who these professionals are:

• "A professional or the professional's delegate who are engaged in the practice of the healing arts, social services, hospital administration, psychological or psychiatric treatment, child care, education, or law enforcement" and clergy as part of their ministerial duties.[14]

• "A professional or the professional's delegate while engaged in: (1) social services; (2) law enforcement; (3) education; (4) the care of vulnerable adults; . . . . (6) an employee of a rehabilitation facility . . .; (7) an employee or person providing services in a facility [licensed to serve adults] . . . ."[15]

Professionals are held to this requirement whether they volunteer or get paid. And even non-professional volunteers could be considered professionals' delegates, making them required to report abuse, too. Therefore, volunteers who could be considered professionals' delegates need adequate training in this area.

Anyone who reports suspected abuse in good faith is immune from liability. However, anyone who knowingly and recklessly makes a false report may be held liable for damages that result from that report.

WHEN BACKGROUND CHECKS ARE REQUIRED FOR VOLUNTEERS

Generally speaking, volunteer organizations do not have to perform background checks on volunteers unless specifically required by a regulation.

Minnesota requires background checks for some volunteers, as well as for others who come in contact with the people a volunteer agency serves.[17] For example, employees who work in stated-licensed facilities fall under this policy. These facilities include group homes, child care centers, adult day care programs, alcohol and drug treatment facilities, and more. Legislation at the federal and state level also encourages voluntary background checks, especially for those programs involving children. Some agencies that are not required to perform background checks have chosen to follow this policy as well because of the intensive roles their volunteers perform with vulnerable people. This is an increasingly accepted practice. Below is a summary of some of this legislation and an explanation of how to get this information. Keep in mind that neither law mandates your organization to conduct a background check.

National Child Protection Act of 1993

This Act requires states to report information on arrests and convictions for child abuse crimes to the National Criminal History Record System (NCHRS) maintained by the Federal Bureau of Investigation. State and local governments had been slow to compile criminal history records and then report such records to the appropriate state and federal authorities.

The act encourages states to improve collection and computerization of their criminal history files, provides for research funds, incentives and penalties related to the transmittal of state criminal records to the NCHRS, and stipulates that state background check requirements may not involve fees that that exceed the actual cost of fingerprinting. It requires that the fees charged to nonprofit entities for background checks do not discourage volunteers from participating in child care programs. The Act also encourages states to enact background check legislation for determining whether a prospective volunteer has been convicted of a crime that bears upon the fitness of individuals who have responsibility for the safety and well-being of children. The decision of whether to enact such legislation is left to the discretion of the states.

Included in the legislative history of the act is this statement: "The (Judiciary) Committee expects that the states, in deciding which types or categories or positions require criminal history background checks, will consider the degree to which a particular position or child care activity offers opportunities to those who would abuse children. The Committee expects... that positions requiring contact with children in one-on-one situations merit a Criminal History Background Check (CHBC) and that positions that involve infrequent direct contact or contact only in group settings do not merit such checks." The Committee also remarks that there are other means available to protect children from abuse, such as investigating the prospective volunteer's employment history and character references and then "properly supervising and training the volunteer."

Minnesota Child Protection Background Check Act (MCPBCA)

This act's purpose is to allow those organizations that provide services to children (and vulnerable adults) to ask that a prospective volunteer submit to a CHBC to determine whether that individual is the subject of a "reported conviction for an enumerated background check crime." An organization requesting such a check must have the informed written consent of the individual before initiating the background check.

In Minnesota, there are two specific types of CHBC. The first is known as the Minnesota Bureau of Criminal Apprehension (BCA) Name Check, which is a search based upon the subject's name and date of birth for offenses committed within and reported to the state of Minnesota. To proceed with a BCA Name Check, the Agency must:

1. Draft a document informing subjects that they will undergo a criminal history search. The document must comply with the dictates of the Minnesota Government Data Practices.

2. Receive the informed consent of the applicant.

3. Forward the signed, notarized application to the BCA.

4. Include a check or money order for $8.00 per applicant.

Within approximately one week of submission, the agency will receive a document detailing the applicant's reported state criminal history. *For copy of this firm see pages 67-70.*

State of Minnesota criminal histories also can be reached in the following ways:

A. BCA Computer Monitor: A computer monitor at the BCA central office is available for use by the public to inspect, in person, at no charge, data collected by the Bureau that identify an individual who was convicted of a crime and the offense for which that person was convicted. Such information is available for a period of fifteen (15) years following the discharge of the sentence imposed. However, the Bureau may charge a fee for copies of the data. By entering the prospective volunteer's exact full name, with or without the date of birth, into the monitor, an agency representative can view conviction data corresponding to the personal information so entered.

B. Local Law Enforcement: Since the summer of 1997, local law enforcement agencies may conduct the BCA name check without paying a fee to the Bureau. However, any information so received must remain private with the Chief of Police or corresponding law enforcement official. Because of the privacy issue, only governmental agencies obtain access to information this way. **If local authorities provide information to non-governmental agencies, they violate state law.**

The second type of search is known as the MCPBCA Statutory or FBI check. This check searches the National Criminal History Records System based upon the applicant's name and fingerprints. To proceed with an FBI check the Agency must:

C. Condsiderations
1. Draft a document informing subjects that their criminal history will be searched. The document must ask the applicant whether they have ever been convicted of any of the enumerated Background

Check Crimes (such as murder or kidnapping) and include a list of such crimes. The document must also comply with the informed consent provisions of the Minnesota Government Data Practices Act (MGPCA).

2. Receive the informed consent of the applicant.

3. Fingerprint the applicant on FBI cards.

4. Forward the signed application to the BCA.

5. Include a check or money order for $24.00 for each applicant.

Within two or three months the Agency will receive a letter from the BCA stating whether the applicant truthfully completed the application, but not an actual criminal record. Contact the Bureau of Criminal Apprehension, Criminal Justice Information Systems Section, for further details and assistance.

C. Considerations: Before deciding whether your organization should conduct a CHBC upon all or some prospective volunteers, please consider the following factors:

1. Usefulness of Information:

a. Only a small fraction of crimes actually result in an arrest.

b. Of those arrested, only a fraction are actually convicted of an offense, let alone the offense for which they were originally arrested. For example, an arrest for sexual misconduct may result in a conviction for simple assault, or the charges may be dropped altogether.

c. Federal and state arrest and conviction data are far from complete because of inadequate reporting from the states and localities. In Minnesota, a year or more may pass between an arrest and recording of the data in the state system.

2. Organizational Burden:

a. Developing, reviewing and storing documents requires a tremendous amount of staff time and effort.

b. Conducting a CHBC is expensive. Could the funds spent on the CHBC be used more effectively in the screening process?

c. The time frames involved require that rospective volunteers might have to wait weeks or months before they can be screened, let alone placed.

3. Necessity of Information:

a. If the volunteer position does not require one-on- one contact with a client, it might be unnecessary to conduct a CHBC.

b. If the decision to conduct a CHBC is made, each agency must decide whether the data received is relevant or useful. Remember that a prior arrest or conviction might not be a legal or even adequate reason to disqualify a volunteer candidate.

c. A CHBC is but one component in the screening process and does not ensure that a candidate is appropriate, nor will the CHBC, in and of itself, shield the Agency from potential liability.

INVASION OF PRIVACY

It's common for volunteer organizations to collect personal data on the people they serve, and on the volunteers themselves. This data may cover a broad range, including information on a person's education, credit history, political affiliations, past employment, medical history, and much more. Under some circumstances, making this data public could invade someone's right to privacy.

When regulations apply to handling personal data

In Minnesota, the ways volunteer organizations handle personal data is generally not regulated. Often the law assumes that the people involved have agreed to let the organization use this data.

However, some organizations are regulated by the Minnesota Government Data Practices Act (MGDPA), Minn. Stat. ch. 13. This is true for organizations that:

• Are agencies of state or local government, which includes any office, department, division, bureau, commission, authority, district or agency of the state.

• Receive certain funding from the government and are under contract to comply with the MGDPA, or

- Contract with the state or a political subdivision of the state (city, school district, county, etc.). Examples are halfway houses, chemical dependency treatment centers, and group homes for people with mental illness.

The MGDPA regulates ,.the way organizations collect, store, maintain, disseminate and access data. The cornerstone of the Act is the presumption that all data collected is public and accessible by the public for inspection and copying unless there is a federal law or state statute that makes the data not public. It also provides penalties, either by suit or injunction, for violating the statute.

Because a large number of organizations are affected by the Act, below is a summary of certain key provisions that may directly affect the daily operations of your agency.

If your agency meets or seems to meet one or more of the definitions listed above it should operate under the assumption that all the data it collects are public data unless a particular operation of law classifies such data as either non-public, protected non-public, or, with respect to individuals, as private or confidential. These terms are defined below.

1. Non-Public Data: Means data not on individuals that are made by statute or federal law:
   a. not accessible to the public; and
   b. accessible to the subject, if any, of the data. Non-Public data are accessible only by the data subject and agency officials who are exercising duties that require access to such data.

2. Protected Non-Public Data: Means data not on individuals that are made by statute or federal law:
   a. not public; and
   b. not accessible to the individual subject of that data.

3. Private Data on Individuals: Means data that are made by statute or federal law:
   a. not public; and
   b. accessible to the individual subject of that data. Private data on individuals are accessible only

by the data subject and agency officials who are exercising duties that require access to such data.

4. Confidential Data on Individuals: Means data that is made not public by statute or federal law and is inaccessible to the individual subject of the data. Confidential data on individuals are accessible only by agency officials who are exercising duties that require access to such data.

5. Individual: Means a natural person. In the case of a minor or an individual who has been adjudged to be mentally incompetent, the term individual includes a parent or guardian or an individual acting as a parent or guardian in the absence of the parent or guardian. In some instances, data can be withheld from parents or guardians if the data are deemed to be in the best interest of the minor.

6. Data on Individuals: Means all government data in which an individual is or can be identified as the subject of the data, unless the appearance of the name or other identifying data can be clearly demonstrated to be only incidental to the data and the data are not accessed by the name or other identifying data of any individual.

Access to Government Data

1. All government data collected. . .by a state agency. …are presumed to be Public Data, therefore making the data accessible by the general public. It is the responsibility of every state agency or political subdivision. . . to keep records containing government data in such an arrangement and condition so as to make such records easily accessible for convenient use. All photographic, photostatic, micrographic, or microfilmed records are considered accessible for convenient use regardless of the size of such record.

2. The Responsible Authority is the person within the governmental entity responsible for establishing a written procedure to ensure that requests for governmental data are received and complied with in an appropriate and prompt manner. The Responsible Authority (RA) means the individual in each agency who is designated or appointed.

3. Upon a Request for Access to data made upon the RA (or designer), the person making the request must be permitted to inspect and copy public government data at reasonable times and places, and, upon request, must be informed of the data's meaning. No fee may be charged for mere inspection of data.

If the person requests a copy of the data, it must be provided at the time the request was made or within a reasonable period of time.* The RA may impose a fee for each copy (or electronic transmittal) that reflects the actual costs of searching for and retrieving the data, including the cost of employee time, and for making, certifying, compiling, and transmitting the data. However, said fees may not include a charge for separating public from not-public data.

If the RA determines that the requested data is classified so as to deny the requested access to the data, the RA must notify the person of the determination either orally at the time of the request, or in writing as soon after that time as possible, and the RA must cite the specific statutory section, temporary classification, or specific provision of federal law upon which the determination was made.

4. The Classification of Data in the possession of an entity will change if necessary to comply with either judicial or administrative rules pertaining to the conduct of legal actions or with a specific statute that applies to data in the possession of the disseminating or receiving agency.

If government data are disseminated from one state agency to another, or to a political subdivision or statewide system, the disseminated data will retain the same classification in the receiving agency as it had originally.

Rights of Subjects of Data

An agency that seeks to collect private or confidential data from an individual must inform or warn the individual of his or her rights regarding its use. Such information to be given to the data subject is often

referred to as the "Tennessen Warning", named for the Act's original author in the Minnesota Senate, Robert Tennessen.

1. The Tennessen Warning requires that the individual be informed of:

a. The purpose and intended use of the data within the collecting agency. . .;

b. Whether the individual may refuse or is legally required to supply the requested data;

c. Any known consequence arising from supplying or refusing to supply private or confidential data; and

d. The identity of other persons or entities authorized by state or federal law to receive the data.

Please note that the Tennessen Warning is not required when an individual is asked to supply investigative data to a law enforcement officer.

The key aspect is the limitation placed on the entity concerning the use and dissemination of private. Only those persons within the entity who are identified in the Tennessen Warning and whose work (volunteer) assignments reasonably require access the data may see it.

Furthermore, the data collected may be only used by those persons within the entity for the specific legal reasons set forth in the Warning. The only exception to this dictate is the "Informed Consent" provision (See Duties of Responsible Authority, section 2.) An entity may not collect or create private data from an individual if no warning is given.

Although not required by the statute, sound risk management procedure dictates that the Tennessen Warning be given in written form and be acknowledged by the signature of the data subject or the person's legal guardian whenever possible. In cases where such is not possible, a verbal recitation or recorded message may suffice to protect the entity. *(See sample Tennessen Warning below.)*

---

* *See Rights of Subject of data, section 2 below for time period when the request is made by the data subject.*

a. The information requested on the registration form will be used to verify eligibility and determine staff and facility needs.

b. Your child's name, age, telephone number, and medical information will be provided to agency staff; volunteers; and the agency attorney, insurer, and auditor.

c. Although you are not required to disclose this information, failure to do so will prevent your child from participating in the program.

Although this sample was specifically written for a municipal agency, it can serve as the basis for your agency's Tennessen Warning as well.

2. Access to data by the individual subject is required upon a request to the Responsible Authority who the must tell the individual whether he or she is the subject of stored data on individuals, and identify the classification of such data as either public, private or confidential.

Upon further request, an individual who is the subject of stored private or public data on individuals must be shown the data without charge, and if desired, be informed of the content and meaning of those data. The RA may impose a charge for any copies made.

The RA must comply immediately, if possible, with any request or within five business days if immediate compliance is not possible. An additional five business days may be allowed in certain circumstances to comply with the request.

3. If data are inaccurate or incomplete, the individual data subject may contest it by notifying the RA of the nature of the disagreement in writing. Upon receipt of this written disgreement, the RA must either:

a. correct the data and notify past recipients of the inaccurate or incomplete data or

b. notify the individual that the authority believes the data to be correct. Any data on an individual that is successfully challenged by the subject must be completed, corrected, or destroyed by the entity.

Please note that the provisions of the MGDPA also apply to data collected. . . from entity staff, volunteers and job applicants.

Duties of Responsible Authority

Section 5 of the Act sets forth the specific duties of the Responsible Authority of the entity. Among the duties are the following:

1. A Public Document containing the RA's name, title and address, along with a description of each category of record, file, or process relating to private or confidential data on individuals maintained by the entity must be prepared by the RA of each entity. Any forms used to collect private and confidential data must be included in the public document, which must be updated annually.

2. Collection and Storage of all data on individuals and the use and dissemination of such data is limited to the extent necessary for the administration and management of the program in question.

The RA must establish procedures to insure that all data on individuals is accurate, complete, and current for the purposes for which it was collected; and establish appropriate security safeguards for all records containing data on individuals.

3. Collection and use of data is limited. Private or confidential data on an individual may be collected, stored, used, or disseminated by the entity for only those purposes told to the individual at the time the data was collected *(See Tennessen Warning)*, unless additional use is authorized by law or the Commissioner of Administration or the individual gives "Informed Consent".

4. The entity may not disclose private data to a person or agency not identified in the Tennessen Warning unless the subject of the data had given Informed Consent. Informed Consent must be given in a written document that is:

a. in plain language;

b. dated;

c. specific in designating the particular persons or agencies the data subject is authorizing to disclose information about the data subject;

d. specific as to the nature of the information the subject is authorizing to be disclosed;

e. specific as to the persons or agencies to whom the subject is authorizing information to be released;

f. specific as to the purpose or purposes for which the information may be used by any of the parties named in clause (e), both at the times of disclosure and at any time in the future;

g. specific as to its expiration date which should be within a reasonable period of time, not to exceed one year, except in case of authorizations given in connection with applications for life insurance or noncancelable or guaranteed renewable health insurance and identified as such, two years after the date of the policy.

The steps outlined above mirror the dictates of the Tennessen Warning, with the additional requirement that the document include an endorsed and dated writing that lists a specific expiration date. Please note that access to data that is sought through an Informed Consent document remains limited to those persons or agencies as specified in the consent form.

5. Summary data is extracted from statistical records and reports derived from private or confidential data on individuals, from which the individuals cannot be identified. Summary data must be prepared by the RA or a designer upon the written request of any person who pays the cost of preparing such data.

Personnel Data

The MGDPA classifies data regarding persons who work, volunteer for, or apply for work with an entity covered by the statute as "personnel data." Certain information relating to such persons is "public."

1. Personnel data includes data on individuals, collected because the individual is or was an employee of, or an applicant for employment by, or who performs services on a voluntary basis for, or acts as an independent contractor with a state agency, political subdivision, or statewide system, or is an applicant for an advisory board or commission.

2. Public data on current and former employees, volunteers, and independent contractors (employees) of a state agency. . . consists of their name; actual gross salary; salary range; contract fees, actual gross pension; the value and nature of employer-paid fringe benefits; the basis for and the amount of any added remuneration, including expense reimbursement, in addition to salary; job title; job description; education and training background; previous work experience; date of first and last employment, the existence and status of any complaints or charges against the employee, whether or not the complaint or charge resulted in disciplinary action; the final disposition of any disciplinary action together with the specific reasons for the action and data documenting the basis for the action, excluding data that would identify confidential sources who are employees of the public body; the terms of any agreement or buy-out settling any dispute arising out of the employment relationship; work location; a work telephone number; badge number; honors and awards received; payroll time sheets or other comparable data that are used to account for the employee's work time for payroll purposes, except to the extent that release of time sheet data would reveal the employee's reasons for the use of sick or other medical leave or other non-public data; and city and county of residence.

A final disposition occurs when the state agency. . . makes a final decision about the disciplinary action, regardless of the possibility of any later proceedings or court proceedings. Final disposition includes a resignation by an individual when the resignation occurs after the final decision of the state agency. . .

3. Public employment application data in Subdivision 3 states that the following personnel data on current and former applicants for employment by a state agency, political subdivision, or statewide system or appointment to an advisory commission or board is public: veteran status, relevant test scores, rank on eligible list, job history, education and training, and work availability.

However, names of applicants are private data until the applicant is certified as eligible for appointment to a vacancy or when the applicant is considered by the appointing entity to be a finalist for a position in public employment. "Finalist" means an individual who is selected to be interviewed by the appointing entity prior to selection.

Names and home addresses of applicants for appointment to and members of an advisory board or commission are public.

4. Other Personnel Data is private data which may only be released pursuant to court order.

Penalties for Misuse of Data

1. Civil Penalties: A person or representative of a decedent who suffers any damage as a result of a violation of a provision of the Act by a state agency. . . may bring an action against the state agency. . . to cover any damages sustained, plus costs and reasonable attorney's fees. In the case of a willful violation, the state agency. . . may be liable for exemplary damages sustained by the injured party.

In addition to bringing a civil action seeking money damages, the injured party may also seek injunctive relief or bring an action to compel the state agency. . . to comply with the dictates of the Act.

2. Criminal Penalties: Any person who willfully violates the provisions of the Act may be found guilty of committing a misdemeanor offense. In the case of a public employee, such a conviction will constitute just cause for suspension or dismissal.

The MGDPA divides data into several categories. These are based on two questions:

• Is the data on individuals (for example, name, sex, or employment records)?

• Or is the data not on individuals (for example, financial records)?

These two categories are then divided according to the access allowed to the data. The following chart summarizes that access:

HOW THE MGDPA CLASSIFIES DATA

Data on Individuals

Type of Data	Access allowed
Public	Open to inspection
Private	Open to the subject of the data and to officials authorized by law to have access
Confidential	Accessible only to officials who use the data

Data Not on Individuals

Type of Data	Access Allowed
Public	Open to inspection
Non-public	Open to the subject of the data and to officials authorized by law to have access
Protected	Accessible only to officials authorized by law to have access

Consider the risk of invading privacy

One more concern is relevant here. Some volunteer organizations do not have systems to control access to personal data. These organizations are generally not liable for publishing such data. At this time, the Minnesota Supreme Court does not recognize invasion of privacy as an injury that merits compensation.[18] However, most other states do recognize invasion of privacy claims, and litigants in Minnesota keep trying to change the law. In a recent case, the Minnesota Court of Appeals reluctantly followed the Minnesota Supreme Court, but said it could not see any good reason for Minnesota not to recognize a claim for invasion of privacy.[19] In one case that got around the invasion of privacy claims, the Minnesota Court of Appeals decided that a physician could be held liable for a breach of an implied contract to keep a client's records confidential.[20] These cases signal a growing push on the Minnesota Supreme Court to change the law on invasion of privacy. Therefore, you should be careful about revealing private information, or making statements that may viewed as contracts about how data will be handled if the data are not government data. Most volunteer organizations use, collect, and disseminate data. And even if an organization is not required to conform to the Minnesota Governmental Data Practices Act, it needs to control access to such data. When creating a data control system, consider the specific needs and goals of your organization. Then get specific advice from your legal counsel.

SUMMARY OF PART ONE

Today it's a fact that charitable organizations can be sued. And some of the most common legal issues faced by such organizations regard volunteers. By involving volunteers, these organizations can become liable for injury to a third person.

Four areas are of particular concern: Negligence, strict liability, intentional misconduct and criminal conduct, and invasion of privacy rights.

It's also essential for any organization to carefully choose and monitor volunteers especially those who come in contact with vulnerable people.

PART TWO

Part Two focuses on two types of liability that can spring from the day-to-day operations of a volunteer organization. These relate to:

• Duties of the organization's directors and officers

• Issues that arise from terminating a volunteer

Other business liability questions exist, but they are beyond the scope of this guidebook: tax issues, pension issues, benefit issues, and more. For other materials on these topics, see page 73.

DUTIES OF YOUR DIRECTORS AND OFFICERS

Directors and officers (board members) of a nonprofit organization or a volunteer program have certain duties. Among them are to see that the organization or program is run in a business/like manner. Of special note are duty of care, duty of loyalty, and duty of obedience.

Note: Committee members of an organization are considered directors only for the purposes of the duties of care and loyalty.[21] Who, specifically, is a committee member? This should be defined in the by laws for your organization. The duties of care and loyalty owed by committee members are the same owed by directors and officers.

Duty of care

Minnesota law sets out a general standard of acting in good faith--a standard that falls under the duty of care:[22]

> "A director shall discharge the duties of the position of director in good faith, in a manner the director reasonably believes to be in the best interests of the corporation, and with the care an ordinarily prudent person in a like position would exercise under similar circumstances. A person who so performs those duties is not liable by reason of being or having been a director of the corporation."

Under this standard, directors and officers have a duty to act in an honest manner, and in the best interest of the program. For instance, a small organization has funds to create one new staff position. The directors and officers comply with the duty of care if they hire one qualified person for the job. However, if they hire three people without an adequate source of funds, then they violate this duty.

Directors and officers also have the duty of attention, another aspect of the duty of care. Among other things, the duty of attention means attending meetings regularly, reviewing relevant information, and generally taking the organization's or program's makers seriously. What does the term "seriously" mean in this context? Some answers are: taking care in selecting staff, objecting to courses of action that appear unwise, establishing organizational goals, and monitoring progress toward those goals. In short, a director must be more than a figurehead or rubber stamp for the decisions of an organization.

The law provides protection from liability for volunteers who act on behalf of a nonprofit corporation, including directors and officers who serve without compensation.[23] In one recent case, the Minnesota Supreme Court applied this protection to a veterinarian who voluntarily served as a director on the board of the humane society.[24] The veterinarian had recommended a type of cleaning chemical to be used to clean animal cages, and an employee of the humane society claimed he had been injured by the chemical. The Court found that the veterinarian had acted in good faith, and was therefore protected by the law from liability. The Court gave the director this protection even though recommending cleaning chemicals did not technically fall within the scope of the veterinarian's duties as a director.

Duty of loyalty

A second duty of directors and officers is the duty of loyalty. This concerns avoiding conflicts of interest, and keeping the best interests of the organization in mind. Minnesota law sets out specific rules regarding conflicts of interest.[25]

Say that an organization wants to expand and move to a new, larger office building. One of the organization's board members knows of a suitable space and decides to buy it. This board member then sells it back to the organization for a profit. Here is one clear instance of a conflict of interest.

Avoiding such conflicts is crucial. Technical conflicts of interest can arise even when directors do not personally benefit from their relationship to an organization. Make sure any decision involving a director is fair to the organization. A recommended policy is to avoid even the appearance of a conflict of interest.

Confidentiality is also important to the duty of loyalty. A director, officer, or board member should not discuss certain organizational business with people outside the organization. This business could include, for example, information on personnel, people served by the agency, litigation, and finances.

One final point: The Minnesota Supreme Court has decided that managers of nonprofits owe the same duties of care and loyalty as directors of private corporations. Nonprofit managers are also charged with the same fidelity in performing their duties as their counterparts in private corporations.[26]

Duty of Obedience

A third duty of directors and officers is to perform their duties in accordance with the applicable statutes and the terms of the organization's bylaws. In addition to observing the formalities and separate existence of the organization, the directors and officers must obey the laws that may impose liability upon them for wrongful conduct. Examples would be: Employment Retirement Income Security Act (ERISA) claims, copyright patent claims, employment practices claims, Nonprofit Corporation Act (Minnesota Statutes, Chapter 317A).

ISSUES THAT ARISE FROM TERMINATING A VOLUNTEER

Making sure that directors and officers exercise their duties of care and loyalty is one way to control your organization's legal liabilities. However, there is still another source of potential liability that deserves your consideration.

Sometimes volunteers are not able to meet the requirements for their position, and they are "terminated". Although these people are not employees, they may still have some legal remedies available. There are laws, such as those against discrimination and governing people with disabilities, that protect terminated volunteers for public policy reasons. The courts have been inconsistent in interpreting these laws as they apply to volunteers, and we can expect changes in the future. Even so, it's advisable to honor the ethic of Equal Employment Opportunity statutes when terminating volunteers.

As mentioned earlier, volunteers are often being defined as gratuitous employees. In fact, the trend by courts and administrative bodies is, for personnel purposes, to treat volunteers like employees. It's also recognized that volunteers should receive similar treatment as paid staff. Indeed, volunteer administrators are increasingly becoming part of many management teams.

The result: Similar systems for managing employees and volunteers are appropriate for your organization-- even necessary. Job descriptions for volunteers become important, especially when issues of liability arise. If an injury results from a volunteer's acts but those acts are outside the job description, your organization might not be held liable.

Preparing volunteers for their responsibilities is also crucial. Appropriate training and orientation means that volunteers are less likely to act in ways that make your organization liable. And if injury does result from a volunteer's actions, evidence of training can establish that the volunteer--not your organization --is liable.

In short, it's wise to develop policies and procedures for hiring and firing volunteers–just as you would for employees. However, be careful. Such policies and procedures might lead courts to interpret them as contracts. If those contracts are violated, the volunteer may have the right to sue for damages. Get careful guidance from your legal counsel in this area.

SUMMARY OF PART TWO

Directors and officers of an organization involving volunteers have certain legal duties.
These fall under two main categories:

• The duty of care--the responsibility to act in an honest manner and in the best interests of the
organization. Related to this is the duty of attention, which means that officers must take the
operation of the organization seriously and fully take part in its decisions.

• The duty of loyalty--the responsibility to avoid conflicts of interest and keep appropriate
information confidential.

• The duty of obedience--the responsibility to follow organizational documents and applicable
local, state and federal statutes.

In addition, legal issues can arise from terminating a volunteer. In order to avoid this risk,
consider hiring, training, supervising, and "firing" volunteers with the same care you would
with employees.

PART THREE

DEFENSES YOU CAN USE IF YOU ARE SUED

In this section we will discuss various defenses that volunteers and volunteer organizations can use if they are sued for personal injury. Topics included are:

• Waivers: The injured person agrees not to hold you liable

• Assumption of risk: The injured person assumes responsibility

• Comparative or contributory negligence: The injured person assumes partial responsibility

• Protection under the State Tort Claims Act

• Protection under other legislation

• What to do if you are sued

WAIVERS: THE INJURED PERSON AGREES NOT TO HOLD YOU LIABLE

Waivers are one way that an organization might escape liability. These are essentially contracts between an organization and the person it serves. With a waiver, the person being served agrees not to hold the organization or its volunteers liable in case of injury or other damages. Waivers are also called exculpatory contracts.

To be effective, waivers must be put in writing and signed before the organization or volunteer renders the service. Be aware, however, that waivers do not hold up well in court. Some of the factors that courts look at include:

• Is there equal power between the parties to the agreement? If so, it is more likely to be enforced. In some cases that involve parties without equal power, like a travel agent and an airline, courts will not enforce waivers. Minnesota will not enforce waivers between employers and employees because of the unequal bargaining power.[27]

• Is the organization offering a public or essential service? If so, a court will not enforce the waiver. When deciding whether the service is public, a court will look at whether it is a necessity for the person receiving the service. For example, the Minnesota Supreme Court considers hospitals, hotels, public utilities and common carriers to be examples of organizations that provide public services.[28] The Court does not consider recreational activities to be public services.

• Is the waiver limited to damages caused by negligence, or does the waiver include intentional acts? Courts in Minnesota will only enforce a waiver that is limited to negligence. Courts will not enforce a waiver that goes beyond negligence and includes intentional acts.[29]

• Is the waiver vague or does it clearly state what claims are being waived? A waiver must clearly define what is being waived by the individual signing it. A vague or ambiguous waiver will not be enforced.

For example, in one Minnesota case, an individual signed a waiver at a health club that waived any claims for injuries caused by the negligence of the health club, "or otherwise." The court found that the "or otherwise" language was too ambiguous and could include injuries caused by intentional acts. The court said that ambiguity made the waiver unenforceable.[30]

• Did the individual have a reason to expect that the waiver included the particular activity that caused the injury? If so, a court is more likely to enforce the waiver. For example, a Minnesota court dismissed a claim that a skydiving club had negligently packed a parachute because the person signed a waiver for the skydiving lesson, and packing the parachute was a part of the service.[31] In contrast, a court refused to enforce a waiver in a case where an individual was injured when he inhaled harmful vapors at a health club because the injury had nothing to do with the individual's use of the club.[32]

Two examples of waivers that were enforced by Minnesota courts are included in the Appendix. Following this format may assist you in drafting a waiver, but it does not mean that the waiver will be enforced. As explained above, courts look at many different factors and must analyze those factors in the particular circumstance involved.

Do not confuse waivers with releases and authorizations. The latter two documents are more limited and specific than waivers. And even with releases and authorizations, legal liability can still exist.

Releases are signed documents granting permission to do something. When parents sign a document allowing their children to go on a school field trip, they are signing a release. This permits the children to go on the trip, but will not exempt supervisors from their duty of care if an accident should happen. When obtaining a release from a parent or guardian, it is important to specify the particular activity involved. For example, the release should say the parent gives permission to take the child to the zoo, rather than just generally saying the child can go on a field trip.

Authorizations are also signed documents giving permission for something. For example, a television producer may seek permission to include taped interviews in a documentary. Normally the producer will ask the people who were interviewed to sign authorizations. These people, however, could still sue for libel if they felt the documentary as a whole damaged their reputations.

ASSUMPTION OF RISK: THE INJURED PERSON ASSUMES RESPONSIBILITY

This defense rests on simple logic. Suppose that injured persons know of the risk of injury and voluntarily put themselves in a situation where injury is likely. In this case, they assume the risk and the responsibility for their own injuries. As an example, consider the person who volunteers to rescue someone in a wilderness area. This person knows that the rescue could be dangerous and is therefore assuming the risk.

COMPARATIVE OR CONTRIBUTORY NEGLIGENCE: THE INJURED PERSON ASSUMES PARTIAL RESPONSIBILITY

How comparative negligence works

Comparative negligence makes injured persons responsible for the portion of their injuries that result from their own negligence.

The best example of comparative negligence is a three-car accident where all the drivers have been negligent in some way. Under Minnesota law, damages in these cases are decided according to fault of each driver, as determined by a jury.[33] Each driver is then liable to the other drivers for damages. (This is called joint and several liability.) The driver who pays the whole award can collect from the other drivers their share of the award.

Consider an accident in which there is a $10,000 award for injuries. Driver A is found to be 50% negligent and Driver B is 20% negligent. Driver C, who is injured, is 30% negligent. Driver A owes $5,000 of the award to driver C, and Driver B owes $2,000 of the award to Driver C. Under joint and several liability, however, Driver C could collect the whole $7,000 from either A or B. Then whoever pays the $7,000 could collect the appropriate share from the other driver.

There are vast differences from state to state in this area. For example, states differ in the way they calculate comparative negligence.

One important note: Comparative negligence will not completely release the organization or volunteer from damages to the injured person. However, this defense can reduce the damages that injured persons receive.

How contributory negligence works

Some states use contributory negligence. According to this concept, the fact that a person contributes to negligence bars that person from collecting anything for injuries. (The state of Minnesota uses comparative negligence--not contributory negligence.)

PROTECTION UNDER THE STATE TORT CLAIMS ACT

A different question of protection arises when the volunteer is working in a program sponsored by a state agency. Under the State Tort Claims Act, state agencies can become liable for the acts of volunteers.[34] This allows persons to sue the state for the torts of its employees.

People employed by the state include those acting on behalf of the state, whether paid or unpaid, just as though they were employees.[35] For the state to be liable, employees or volunteers must be acting within the scope of their duties.

In addition, the State Tort Claims Act covers a specific class of volunteers: those who take part in a court-referred volunteer program. This program allows people convicted of nonviolent crimes to provide community service at the discretion of the court. People who are injured by one of these volunteers can sue the state.[36]

Often the state will indemnify employees who are sued in the scope of their duties. (To indemnify means to compensate employees for their loss.) Will the state indemnify volunteers the same way that it indemnifies employees? The State Tort Claim Act does not say.

We think a strong case can be made for indemnifying volunteers who work with the state. Indemnification offers an incentive for recruiting volunteers. It protects their personal assets and may cover the costs of defense or litigation. In addition, indemnification can provide financial protection for the people a volunteer serves, as well as other injured persons. Remember, however, that indemnification increases exposure to risk and could mean added costs.

If the state would indemnify volunteers, it would probably apply the same requirements that it applies to employees:

• The tort must be committed within the scope of the volunteer's duties.

• The volunteer must cooperate with the state and provide complete disclosure of what happened. Any volunteer who chooses not to do so is barred from later suing the state for indemnification.

There are a number of exceptions to the State Tort Claims Act. They arise, for example, when the employee is acting to execute a law or agency regulatory rule; when there is a loss other than property damage or personal injury; or when an injury results from using or maintaining the state's recreational system. In these situations, the state will not be held liable.

Another important exception is for discretionary acts. Discretionary acts are based partially or totally on policy decisions made by a person who is authorized to make such decisions. This concept becomes important when a volunteer, such as a board member of a state agency, has power to make policy-level decisions. It's likely that most volunteers are not in a position to take discretionary action. In any case, however, the state will not be held liable. For example, the state will not be held liable for a decision the State Board of Education makes on school curriculum. Nor will the state be liable for a decision that Minnesota Board on Aging makes on grant criteria.

This section has discussed claims against the state of Minnesota. But Minnesota law also applies if the injured person has a claim against a political subdivision, such as city or school district.[37] Under this law, the political subdivision can be held liable for acts of its officers, employees, or agents. (Agents include volunteers.[38]) Though there are also some differences between this law and the State Tort Claims Act, the basic idea is the same. And as with the State Tort Claims Act, there is an exception for discretionary acts. When these acts result in injury, the subdivision will not be held liable.

PROTECTION UNDER OTHER LEGISLATION

Partial immunity

The Minnesota Nonprofit Corporation Act provides some protection against legal liability. More specifically, the law protects directors, officers, members, and agents of a nonprofit corporation who are acting without compensation.[39] The word "agents" in the statute could refer to volunteers. This was the drafters' intent. However, the law is new and still needs to be tested in the court system.

Volunteers involved in some sports-related activities are also exempt from liability.[40] This provision protects voluntary athletic associations, their volunteers and managers, and officials of a sports team organized under a nonprofit charter. The volunteer, manager, or official must be serving without compensation. These associations and people are usually not liable for injuring a player, participant, or spectator during organized competition. However, there are some cases in which these associations or persons can be held liable: if they injure someone through intentional or reckless conduct; or if they injure someone through operating, using, or maintaining a motor vehicle.

Minnesota also protects those organizations that provide perishable food to the elderly or the needy.[41] An organization that donates perishable food, and an organization that distributes that perishable food to the elderly or the needy will not be liable for any injury unless the injury is caused by gross negligence, recklessness or intentional misconduct. Gross negligence is different from ordinary negligence. Ordinary negligence involves an inadvertent mistake or lack of attention. Gross negligence, on the other hand, takes place when a person is reckless or indifferent to the duty of care.

Nonprofit organizations that organize events with livestock, such as horses, are not liable for injuries to participants arising out of the "inherent risks" of the livestock activities.[42] "Inherent risks" include kicking, biting or bucking. This protection from liability only covers participants, not spectators. The law requires the organization to post notices that are easy to read to warn participants about the inherent risks of the activity, and to warn participants about the limitation of liability.

Minnesota's Good Samaritan Law gives some protection to the person who helps out in an emergency.[43] The person giving assistance has general immunity from liability--unless that person acts in a reckless or malicious manner. (General immunity means that a person or organization cannot be held liable.) Any immunity applies only to people acting in a voluntary capacity.

In any case, volunteers can still be held liable if they injure others through deliberate, willful misconduct, or if they act in ways that directly result in personal injury. Moreover, the attorney general and federal government can still sue for breach of fiduciary duty. (A fiduciary is a person who occupies a position of trust, especially someone who manages the affairs of another person.)

Volunteer Protection Act of 1997

After 10 years of consideration by Congress, the Volunteer Protection Act of 1997 (VPA) was passed and went into effect mid September, 1997. While the purpose of the act is to address the fear of lawsuits against volunteers, the result has been to raise more questions than it answers. The VPA was written so that it would prempt any state law, unless state law provided additional protection. As of the printing of this book, there has been no analysis of how the VPA will fit with the provisions of Minnesota law. The VPA does allow for the state legislature to opt out of the federal law, but that would only apply if all the parties are citizens of the state. If they are from different states, then the federal law applies. As of

the printing of this book, following the 1998 legislative session, no action has been taken to address these issues. To learn more call the Minnesota Office of Citizenship and Volunteer Services.

Indemnification

Another provision of the Nonprofit Corporation Act requires a nonprofit organization to indemnify its directors, officers, and board committee members, unless its articles or bylaws specifically limit indemnification. The organization will pay the costs and attorney fees of a suit against a director, officer, or committee member. These people must be sued in relation to their duties and must have acted in good faith.

This statute appears to cover only volunteers who are officers or members of the board of directors. Nonprofit organizations can indemnify other volunteers if they wish, but they are not required to. Even so, this act provides guidelines for indemnifying any volunteers who are sued while performing volunteer duties.[44] Remember that volunteers in public agencies are indemnified.

WHAT TO DO IF YOU ARE SUED

If your organization is sued, you must contact an attorney immediately. A lawsuit begins when a party files a document called a complaint with the court. It is then served on the defendants with a document called a summons. There are very strict deadlines for responding to a lawsuit, and the time can be short, such as 20 days after the organization receives the complaint.

When a corporation is sued, an attorney must act on behalf of the corporation. The law does not allow an officer or director or employee to act on behalf of the corporation in court. Only an attorney can represent the corporation during the lawsuit. Although an individual can represent himself or herself, there are many defenses and procedures that can be complicated and require the expertise of a lawyer.

SUMMARY OF PART THREE

Volunteers and volunteer organizations have at least five main lines of defense if they're sued for personal injury:

• Waivers, where the injured person agrees not to hold you responsible.

• Assumption of risk, where the injured person assumes responsibility.

• Comparative or contributory negligence, where the injured person assumes partial responsibility.

• Protection under the State Tort Claims Act.

• Protection under other state legislation, including the Minnesota Nonprofit Corporation Act.

Remember, it is vital that you contact an attorney immediately if you receive a lawsuit that has been filed so that you can preserve your defenses.

PART FOUR

PROTECTING YOUR ORGANIZATION THROUGH RISK MANAGEMENT

The purpose of this is to suggest risk management benefits and goals, along with a process you can use to manage risk. Topics covered include:

- The benefits of risk management

- Risk management: An overview of the process

- Steps 1: Identify the risk

- Step 2: Measure the risk

- Step 3: Select methods to control or finance the risk and implement them

- Step 4: Manage claims and losses

- Step 5 : Monitor the risk management program and make necessary changes

- Keeping records for risk management

- Running your everyday operations to manage risk

As you read this section, keep in mind the difference between pure risk and speculative risk. *Pure risk* exists when there is only the chance of loss but no chance of gain–for example, theft. Risk involving the chance of gain or loss, such as investments, are *speculative risks*. Risk management deals with pure risks.

THE BENEFITS OF RISK MANAGEMENT

A volunteer forgets to unplug an electric heater. This causes a fire that destroys the building you occupy, along with all of your equipment and records.

A volunteer steals money or property from your organization. Or, someone steals a volunteer's money or property.

A volunteer driver, without automobile insurance, has an accident. Your organization is held liable and required to cover the loss.

These are examples of the many potential risks that volunteer organizations face. The pages that follow are about how you can respond through risk management.

Risk management is more than buying insurance. Risk management is realizing that your organization will incur some loss. Risk management is taking action how to prevent loss—and planning now to respond when a loss does occur.

A loss could be large or small. It might result from theft of property. It might result from injury to a client or staff member—injury that could result in medical bills or lost wages. Or loss might result from breach of contract, such as wrongfully terminating an employee or volunteer. These are just a few examples.

Through systematically assessing and identifying risks, your organization can protect the people it serves. You can protect the organization's assets—as well as the assets of your volunteers and directors—against loss. You can prevent or minimize accidents. You can decrease risks to your employees and to the public. Moreover, you can reduce or eliminate the uncertainty that comes with operating a volunteer program. In short, risk management is appropriate for any organization involving volunteers. This is true regardless of the organization's size, and whether or not the organization has paid staff who work along with volunteers.

It's safe to say that most organizations have no systematic approach to risk management. It's also probably safe to say that most organizations have suffered few, if any, losses.

So why bother with all of this? Is risk the only factor to consider when undertaking any activity? No. But without risk management, your organization is exposed to losses that can drain its resources or threaten its existence.

Even a relatively small loss--say, $10,000 of computer equipment--can have a significant effect on an organization. That impact is more than just the loss of dollars to replace the equipment--dollars that would then be unavailable to pay staff or to provide direct services. The impact could extend to loss of information and the staff time it takes to reconstruct lost data.

Your organization is different from any other. Therefore your possible exposure to risk is different. Each organization, and each program within the organization, must examine its own operations and use of resources to discover its own risks. Moreover, the costs of risk management will vary, depending on type of insurance purchased, limits of coverage, and other factors.

Each organization must evaluate its own risk tolerance and establish insurance programs that reflect its own financial ability to assume risk.

DEVELOPING A POLICY ON RISK MANAGEMENT

A risk management program begins with a policy statement. Following are two examples. Use them as ways to begin thinking about a risk management policy for your organization.

Again, the following policy statements are only examples. Your organization should compose and adopt its own wording. This can be done through a risk management committee, a manager, or a management team. You can also get assistance from an experienced risk manager. A local insurance agent or attorney might also be helpful. These people might even be willing to help draft the policy statement if you do not have the staff to do so.

• One way to draft a policy statement is to answer these questions:

• What is the mission of our risk management program?

28

- How can the risk management program contribute to the overall mission of our organization?

- What actions can our staff members and volunteers regularly take to manage risk?

- Who will oversee our risk management efforts, and what will be this person's responsibilities? (In smaller organizations, the position of executive director, business manager, management team or another position may have the delegated duties of the risk manager and the safety director.)

Some policy statements are long and detailed. Yours need not be. For example, specific goals and tasks for risk management can come later, as part of your strategic planning. The crucial point is to start transforming risk management from a "good idea" into a working reality.

Sample Policy Statement #1

The Mission

Our risk management mission is to reduce the costs of pure risks, including premiums and losses. We will use the tools of risk analysis, risk control, and risk finance to carry out this mission.

The Policy

This policy applies to pure risks such as fire, liability, theft, workers compensation, and other direct and indirect risks of property and liability loss. It does not apply to employee benefits costs that are deliberately assumed or speculative risk ventures.

This organization will have a risk manager to direct and coordinate all risk functions. The risk manager is responsible for:

- Analyzing risk

- Selecting risk management methods

- Selecting insurance agents, brokers, and insurance companies

- Purchasing insurance

- Settling claims

The risk manager will coordinate information and offer advice on fire protection, safety, security, and risk involved in contracts and other legal documents.

The organization will have a safety director to implement safeguards that protect employees, volunteers, and the public.

The organization's legal department (or legal counsel) is responsible for all contract wording. However, all contracts that involve insurance, indemnity, or other risk provisions shall be cleared with the risk manager unless circumstances make this impossible.

All organization planning will include a risk assessment to identify potential risks and the means of treating them.

The executive director and all project managers will conduct operations according to organization standards and statutory requirements. They will determine the degree of protection needed for new projects only after review of the plans by the risk manager. They will report all claims, regardless of size, to the risk manager or the designated claim office.

Risk Retention

Losses that individually do not exceed $500 will normally be retained without insurance. Risks with greater potential loss will normally be insured. The risk manager may make exceptions to this rule. All exceptions will be reported to the executive director. (Governmental units or programs subject to governmental regulation may need to follow other guidelines.)

Communications

The risk manager and safety director will be aware of all organization activities. They will visit all organization locations and projects.

The executive director and all project managers will notify the risk manager and safety director of new property values, disposal of assets, and changes in operations.

Indemnification

The organization will indemnify to the extent permitted by law any person made a party to a lawsuit. This includes persons threatened with any action, civil or criminal, due to serving as a director, officer, employee, or volunteer. Sometimes directors, officers, employees, or volunteers will serve on the board of another organization or work or volunteer in some other capacity as part of their duties. Indemnification will extend to these people as a result of these duties.

The risk manager will monitor contracts, assuring that conditions under which the organization is asked to give indemnification or hold-harmless agreements to other parties are appropriate and insurable.

In some contracts, the risk manager may recommend that the organization should request a hold-harmless agreement from the other parties. Here again, the hold-harmless conditions should be appropriate and insurable by the other parties. The risk manager will ask the other parties to submit evidence of insurance (certificates).

Risk Management Committee

The organization will have a risk management committee consisting of its president, chief financial officer, and chief legal officer.

The committee will review all risk management activities. It will receive copies of reports from the risk manager and safety director and make decisions over and above the authority of the executive director, risk manager, and safety director.

The committee shall decide the nature and frequency of risk management audits.

Sample Policy Statement #2

Our organization will apply the risk management process. This process includes systematically and regularly identifying exposures to loss, analyzing these exposures, applying sound risk control procedures, and financing risks.

The goal of risk management is to protect the organization against accidental loss that significantly affects its budget or ability to fulfill its responsibilities. Loss prevention is crucial.

The administration of the risk management program is assigned to the director of risk management, reporting to the executive director.

1. Risk Management Purposes

Objectives:

• Protect against catastrophic losses.

• Minimize the total long-term cost of all activities related to controlling losses.

• Create procedures providing a periodic assessment of exposure to loss, ability to bear loss, and available financial resources, including insurance.

• Establish, as much as possible, an exposure-free environment for clients, employees, and the public.

2. Risk Management Functions

The director of risk management shall have authority to:

• Identify and measure risks of accidental loss.

• Select appropriate techniques for resolving exposure problems

• Risk assumption

• Risk reduction

• Risk retention

• Risk transfer

• Other systems, as appropriate, including the purchase of insurance.

• Develop and maintain a system for the timely and accurate recording of losses, claims, premiums, and other related information.

Allocating insurance premiums, uninsured losses, and other risk costs and information.

3. Risk Retention

With regard to risks of accidental loss it shall be the policy to insure all losses:

• Whenever certain necessary services can be obtained only through the purchase of insurance.

• When obligated by contract or law to purchase insurance.

Generally, your organization will self-insure if economically possible.

4. Purchase of Insurance

Purchase of all property and casualty insurance will be coordinated through the risk manager.

Insurance shall be purchased from any source determined to be in the best interests of the organization.

Whenever possible, agents and brokers providing services will be paid on a fee basis, as opposed to a commission.

Risk Management:
An Overview of the Process

At first, risk management can seem like an overwhelming proposition. Fortunately we can lay out the risk management process in a basic, step-by step format. After developing your policy statement, do the following:

• Step 1: Identify the risk

• Step 2: Measure the risk

• Step 3: Select methods to control or finance the risk and implement them

- Avoid or eliminate the risk
- Reduce the risk
- Transfer the risk control responsibility to other parties
- Retain the risk
- Transfer the finance responsibility to other parties
- Insure the risk: Choosing insurance agents or brokers
- Insure the risk: Choosing insurance companies

• Step 4: Manage claims and losses

- Report claims and losses
- Settle claims and losses
- Keep claims and loss records

• Step 5: Monitor the risk management program and make necessary changes

This outline provides the format for the pages that follow. You'll find a worksheet based on these steps on page first of appendix. Use this worksheet as a way to begin acting on what you read.

Step 1: Identify the risk

Many small organizations do not have a full-time person to coordinate risk management or oversee safety concerns. In this case, the executive director, board chairperson, or someone in a similar leadership position can coordinate risk management and safety planning. For the purposes of the following discussion, this person is called the *risk coordinator.*

This risk coordinator can use tools such as questionnaires, surveys, checklists, and flow charts to identify the risks affecting your organization. Some questions to answer are:

- What is the size of the organization?
- What is the likelihood of an injury or claim?
- What is the risk to the volunteer, and to the people the volunteer comes in contact with?
- What are various risk control methods and their costs?
- Does the volunteer have insurance? If so, what is the extent of coverage?
- Should the volunteer be required to purchase insurance?
- What is the cost of insurance for the volunteer? Should the agency pay the cost?
- If yours is a government agency, does the Minnesota State Tort Claims Act or laws relating to political subdivisions apply to it? (For more information on this topic, see page 23.)
- Do existing insurance policies cover volunteers? If so, in what circumstances? (To answer this question, you may need to review several policies.)
- Does your organization hold special events, such as fund raisers, that increase your risks?
- What are the activities that can give rise to a claim or loss?

- What can I do to minimize or eliminate the risk?

- Does your insurance company provide inspections or surveys? If so, do you review these and implement risk reduction recommendations?

- Does someone review all contracts that your organization is entering into?

- Through contractual arrangements can you assume unexpected liabilities, such as indemnification and hold harmless clauses?

It's essential that your personnel report new activities, projects, and potential risks to the risk coordinator.

For checklists that can help you identify risks, see Part Five of this guidebook.

Step 2: Measure the risk

Risks are measured by attaching dollar figures to them. Here the risk coordinator determines replacement costs for the organization's property. Don't forget intagible risks of damage to image and reputation which can affect the ability to attract resources (dollars, people and property) in the future. It's also important to estimate potential defense, settlement, and judgment costs for liability risks.

Step 3: Select methods to control or finance the risk and implement them

After identifying and measuring the risks your organization faces, the risk coordinator can take steps to control those risks. Some possible steps are explained below.

Avoid or eliminate the risk

The risk coordinator may recommend that the risk management committee avoid or eliminate high-risk projects. An organization, for example, may decide to cancel programs where volunteers take children on hiking, biking, or skiing trips.

Reduce the risk

In this step, the risk coordinator and the safety director implement methods to prevent loss. Keep in mind that loss prevention ordered by governmental or regulatory authorities is compulsory. This is the case, for example, when municipal building codes require you to install handrails on stairways.

Insurers may also recommend ways to prevent loss. With some exceptions, these methods are voluntary.

After an organization identifies and measures its particular risks, ways to prevent losses often become clear. For instance, agencies that frequently use drivers can develop and practice rules for selecting drivers.

Transfer the risk control responsibility to other parties

This step protects people and property before a loss occurs. You could contract with other parties to perform hazardous activities. Then the other party also assumes responsibility for risk of loss. Before your organization moves to another location, for example, you see that lifting heavy items creates an unacceptable risk of injury to your volunteers. In response, you hire a moving company to assume the risk.

Retain the risk

You might decide to retain certain losses as business expenses. That means you plan to pay for them out of your operating expenses. As an example, automobile collision deductibles are usually retained. You could also choose to retain the loss of the entire automobile.

The same practice can be used for any risk that your organization decides to retain. You could, for instance, choose a $1,000 collision deductible for automobiles you own because the premium is much lower than the premium for a $250 collision deductible. In this case, you're retaining the larger deductible.

Transfer the financial responsibility to other parties

Here your organization is protected if and when an actual loss occurs. Consider again the example where you decide to hire a moving company to haul your property to a new location. You could arrange for your moving company to provide full coverage on property being transported to that location.

Insure the risk: Choosing agents or brokers

To handle remaining risks, turn to commercial insurance companies. Before you contact an agent or broker to purchase insurance, understand the types of coverage available:

- General liability insurance (accident/personal liability insurance) covers personal injury and property damage to others resulting from a volunteer's actions.

- Professional insurance protects against claims of wrongful actions by volunteers. Such coverage applies, for example, if a volunteer provides mental health counseling and is subsequently sued for providing inappropriate advice--advice that injures the person who received it.

- Auto insurance protects against damage or bodily injury that results when a volunteer operates a motor vehicle.

- Directors and officers insurance protects the members of your board of directors against claims other than those already described. Typically this coverage applies to breach of fiduciary responsibilities, or actions resulting in financial loss to the organization. Examples include embezzlement of funds or non-payment of taxes.

Even with directors and officers insurance that applies to individuals, your organization could still be sued separately. To protect against such loss, ask your agent or broker about *entity coverage*. This coverage applies to both defense costs and damages.

Next, understand how agents and brokers work. These people place insurance with companies that employ them exclusively, or with companies they represent as independent contractors. Agents and brokers are paid by a commission (part of the insurance premium) or by a fee billed to your organization. Fees are rare, usually charged only for special services beyond evaluating and placing the insurance.

Choose agents and brokers who know about insurance and risk management for volunteer organizations. Other volunteer organizations may be able to recommend specific agents or brokers. When you contact them, ask about their experience in handling insurance for nonprofit and volunteer organizations.

Expect your agents or brokers to evaluate your organization's insurance needs, offer alternative coverages, and recommend companies to provide the insurance. Report any claims to the agent or broker, who will notify the insurer and assure that the claim is adjusted.

Be aware that any application for insurance is a part of the insurance contract. Included as part of the application is any supplemental information required. Complete accuracy and truthfulness is essential. *Misrepresentations, inaccuracies, or false information may void the insurance coverage.* This is especially important when purchasing professional or malpractice insurance and directors and officers insurance.

Agents and brokers have certain duties to your organization. Some of them are:

- Understanding your insurance needs and requirements.

- Explaining alternatives and choices for insurance. (It is your duty to determine values and choose amounts of insurance.)

- Checking the accuracy and completeness of applications for insurance before sending them to insurers. (It is your duty to furnish accurate and complete information for applications.)

- Confirming in writing all oral questions and information from you. Levels and extent of coverage may vary, depending on the insurance company and your sophistication in purchasing insurance.

- Explaining the coverage to you in writing. This means answering questions such as: What is covered? What is excluded? (Exclusions are losses that the policy does not cover.) What other limitations or restrictions apply to this coverage?

- Providing prompt confirmation to you, in writing, of the insurer's agreement to issue coverage.

- Providing a written binder and telling you when the policies will be delivered.

- (A binder is a document that guarantees insurance coverage while the actual policies are being prepared.)

- Verifying the policies for agreement with your order and having the insurer correct discrepancies.

- When the policy is renewed, providing coverage with similar or better terms than the expiring policies. The agent or broker should inform you of all material changes expected on the renewal, or if an insurer refuses to renew within a reasonable time before the renewal date.

- Keeping you informed of material changes in the financial condition of your insurers. The agent or broker should avoid insurers whose financial condition is unstable or uncertain.

- Giving you prompt acknowledgment of claims you report.

- Notifying insurers promptly of all claims that you report.

- Checking progress toward claim settlement by the insurer and informing you of that progress.

- Maintaining claim statistics for your account.

- Informing you when there are indications that an insurer may cancel your policies.

- Informing you whether canceled policies can be replaced, and the terms of the replacement policies.

Ask any agent or broker to deliver evidence of professional liability insurance. At the minimum, the amount of such insurance should equal the total amount of insurance your organization places.

Insure the risk: Choosing insurance companies

Expect your agent or broker to choose insurers offering broad coverage, competitive premium cost/loss control services, and prompt claim settlement.

Again, agents and brokers must assure you that proposed insurers are always financially able to deliver the protection promised by the insurance policy. Ask for information on the financial condition of proposed insurers. This information can come from a variety of sources: copies of articles from Consumer Reports or other financial magazines, reports from independent companies who rate insurance companies (Alfred M. Best, Inc. and Standard & Poors), reports from Minnesota Department of Commerce, or similar sources. The Minnesota Insurance Information Center can also provide information on insurers.

Reports on insurers are not always easy to read, so ask your agent or broker to explain them to you. Seek additional assistance, especially if the information you get is difficult to understand, or if it indicates problems with your insurance company.

Any agent or broker should agree to replace insurers that become unsound before your agency suffers any uninsured loss.

Step 4: Manage claims and losses

As mentioned earlier, risk management assumes that claims and losses will occur. It's vital that your organization manage them efficiently. Taking the actions listed below can help you do so.

Report claims and losses

All insurance policies include specific requirements for reporting claims and losses. Prompt, accurate reporting is required to assure recovery on claims. That's why it's important to report losses immediately. In addition, periodically review claim reports to determine how to eliminate or minimize claims.

Laws and regulations require that your report certain accidents, injuries, and damages to governmental units. Examples are automobile accidents resulting in injury and automobile accidents when damage exceeds a certain amount. (Get details of this requirement from your agent or broker.)

It's your risk coordinator's job to become acquainted with your insurance policies and legal and regulatory requirements. This person should also create procedures to assure prompt reporting.

Settle claims and losses

All insurance policies have terms and conditions for settling claims and losses. Your risk coordinator must know them and monitor the progress of all claims and losses.

Other duties of the risk coordinator in this area include:

- Making sure that your organization's personnel cooperate fully in settling all claims and losses.

- Assuring that agents, brokers, and insurers provide necessary service, and that they settle claims and losses according to policy provisions.

- Working with your legal department to assure that claims against third parties are pursued and recoveries are made.

It is a good idea to have one person in an organization designated to be responsible for handling lawsuits that are served or threatened. A corporation cannot represent itself; it must have a lawyer appear in court and respond to court papers. Because of strict time deadlines for responding to a lawsuit, it is important to contact a lawyer as soon as possible. Designating one person with the responsibility for obtaining the lawyer will help prevent missed deadlines.

Keep claim and loss records

The risk coordinator should maintain accurate records of all incidents, accidents, occurrences, injuries, damages, claims, and losses. Such information is essential for effective risk identification. New insurers require full information on past claims and losses, so retain these records permanently.

You'll find a sample accident report form on page 74 to assist with this task.

Step 5: Monitor the risk management program and make necessary changes

Risk management is a process, a way of thinking. That means it's never finished. After your risk management program is in place, evaluate it at regular intervals. The best way to organize this effort is simply to cycle again through the first four steps explained above. In addition, your organization's experience with claims and losses will give you direct feedback on how well your program is working.

More specifically, answer these questions:

- How effective are risk controls we put in place?

- If we retained any risks, is it wise for us to keep doing so?

- Is our insurance program adequately helping us manage our risks?

- What specific changes do we want to make in our risk management program?

- How much will any changes cost?

- How will we implement any changes?

Review incident and loss reports to identify problem areas and causes of loss prevent repetition of these claims.

KEEPING RECORDS FOR RISK MANAGEMENT

Step 4 of our risk management model underlines how important it is to keep records of claims and losses. This step calls for further explanation. More specifically, to keep effective records you can:

- Review insurance policies and endorsements

- Store and retain policies safely

- Keep claim and loss records

More details about each of these actions follows.

Maintain risk information

The risk coordinator should maintain all information on risks as permanent records. This includes information in any form, such as surveys, checklists, and flow charts. Use your records as the source of accurate information for insurance applications requested by agents or insurers. Keep all applications with the surveys, and add information on new risks.

In Section Five you'll find checklists that can help you maintain information on certain risks.

Review insurance policies and endorsements

When your agent or broker delivers binders, policies, endorsements, or riders, be sure to do the following:

- Check the accuracy of your organization's name, address, and the description of the property or liability covered.

- Review the policy. Ask your agent or broker to explain the insuring agreement, exclusions, deductible, and policy conditions.

- Determine whether the policy offers claims made coverage or occurrence coverage. *Claims made coverage* only applies to an injury or loss that occurs during the policy period and is reported to the insurance company during the policy term or the "extended reporting period" as provided in the policy. Usually this is a limited period of 30 to 90 days. It is possible for an additional premium to buy an "extended reporting period" to extend the time limits to report a claim to the insurance company. This is a more common form of coverage today. *Occurrence coverage* provides protection for any injury or loss that occurred during the period covered by the policy–regardless of when the claim is actually made. The difference between these two types of coverage can be crucial, especially if you change insurance companies.

- Ask the agent to explain your organization's duties under the policy.

- Have the agent explain how any endorsement affects coverage. An *endorsement,* sometimes called a *rider,* modifies the terms of the basic policy. All endorsements should be permanently attached to your policy.

Store and retain policies safely

Treat all insurance policies as valuable records. If possible, store policies in fire-resistant cabinets.

Some losses may not be discovered until after the policy expires. This makes it essential to retain all insurance policies for a certain number of years following expiration. This period varies. Ask your agent or broker how many years after expiration you should retain each type of policy.

Keep claim and loss records

Retain copies of all claim reports submitted under your organization's insurance coverage. You will need this information to discuss a claim settlement. Claim records are also vital for reviewing your risk management program. Retain these as permanent records.

Volunteers or employees might have an accident with their own vehicles while working for your organization.

If they do, make sure they report the accident to their insurers and, when required, to the state. Your organization may want this information on file also.

RUNNING YOUR EVERYDAY OPERATIONS TO MANAGE RISK

All persons connected with your organization are part of the risk management process. To help them be an effective part of that process, review with them the basic principles discussed below.

Help the risk coordinator identify risks

Your risk coordinator may interview various people to identify volunteer organization risks. In addition, your organization's managers, employees, and volunteers must inform the risk coordinator of new activities and risks.

Take part in safety programs

Ask your safety director to train your staff and volunteers in preventing loss and accidents; include safe driving practices. Document that this training took place. Also make sure that these people observe safe working practices.

Report claims and losses

Persons involved in losses can obtain a claim form and report complete details of the loss to the risk coordinator, or to the designated claim office. Your organization's policies and procedures will determine appropriate time frames for submitting reports. Coordinate these procedures with your insurance and, in cases such as workers' compensation, with governmental requirements.

In effective risk management, all personnel cooperate in settling a claim or loss, as requested by the risk coordinator.

Obtain evidence of insurance

The actions you take here will vary with the type of insurance involved.

Your organization may be held responsible for injuries and damages caused by volunteers using their own motor vehicles on organization business. Ask these volunteers to have their insurance companies issue certificates of automobile insurance to your organization. Be sure to get new certificates when the insurance is renewed.

Your organization might be served by volunteer or employed professionals such as lawyers, physicians, or accountants. If so, there is a risk of professional liability. You may want to ask all professionals to have their insurers issue certificates of professional liability to your organization. Also ask them to order new certificates when the professional liability insurance is renewed.

If you hire independent contractors to perform services for you, be sure to obtain certificates of Workers' Compensation insurance before they are allowed to work on the premises.

Examine leases and other contracts

Many volunteer organizations have leases covering their responsibilities as tenants or landlords.

Carefully examine all leases. They may impose unreasonable or uninsurable responsibility for injuries and damages. Your organization's legal counsel and risk coordinator should review all leases for equity and insurability.

Do the same with contracts, including construction contracts, supply contracts, and purchase orders. Again, all contracts should be reviewed by the attorney and risk coordinator.

Why go to this trouble? Because when you hire independent contractors, you might be responsible for injuries or damages caused by their negligence. Suppose, for example, that a building contractor is installing partitions in your office. If a partition falls and injures one of your clients, your organization could be held liable.

Ask independent contractors to have their insurers issue certificates of insurance to your organization. Normally you will want certificates of general liability, automobile liability, and workers' compensation insurance before contractors begin work. The nature of the work done by the independent contractor may require that you get other certificates as well. Discuss the circumstances with your attorney and your agent or broker.

SUMMARY OF PART FOUR

One of the most effective ways to protect your organization financially and legally is a sound program to manage risks. This begins with developing an official policy on risk management. Then put your policy into action by following the five basic steps of risk management:

- **Step 1: Identify the risk**

- **Step 2: Measure the risk**

- **Step 3: Select methods to control or finance the risk and implement them**

- **Step 4: Manage claims and losses**

- **Step 5: Monitor the risk management program and make necessary changes**

Also essential to risk management is keeping adequate records and running your every-day operations to manage risk.

PART FIVE

SOME SPECIAL RISKS YOUR ORGANIZATIONS MIGHT FACE

PREVIEW OF PART FIVE

This section addresses some risks that are of special concern to the volunteer organization:

• Personnel issues

• Automobile liability

• Directors and officers liability

• General liability

• Liability associated with vulnerable volunteers

• Professional and malpractice liability

• Offering services to vulnerable people

• Workers compensation

• Other issues that can affect your volunteer program

Keep in mind that the risks just mentioned are merely examples. Your risk coordinator is encouraged to carefully analyze other risks affecting your organization. Page 64 includes a list of such additional risks. These are concerns for the volunteer activity of any organization, and for the organization as a whole.

Much of the text in this section consists of checklists for risk management. Their purpose is to help your organization move from planning into action. Each item on these checklists identifies a possible risk for your organization, or an issue related to such risk. Completing each checklist will bring the next steps in your risk management program into clearer focus.

Again, these checklists are only a starting point. None of them is meant to lay down policy or set out standards. They are included to stimulate your thinking. Each organization is unique. Your own risk evaluation will identify other areas of concern, as will your agent and insurers. To get the most benefit from this section, go through all of the following checklists. Then design others to fit your own organization.

PERSONNEL ISSUES

The following questions point out broad liability concerns that relate to volunteers. Note that many of these questions apply to almost any organization or type of volunteer.

Job descriptions

❏ Does the volunteer job description indicate what qualifications are necessary?

❏ Is professional insurance required for the person in this position?

❏ Is it provided by the agency or the individual?

❏ Are there physical requirements for the position (height, weight, etc.)?

❏ Has our organization reviewed the job description with Equal Employment Opportunity concerns (protection against discrimination) in mind?

> *Note: Federal, state, and local municipalities have different categories of Equal Employment Opportunity coverage. Determine what jurisdictions cover your agency. In addition, coverages not required may be added to your agency's criteria.*

Volunteer file

❏ Do we use applications to screen volunteers?

> *Note: The Equal Employment Opportunity concerns described above also apply here.*

❏ Do we review volunteer performance?

❏ Do we have a system for handling complaints against volunteers?

❏ Do we have formal procedures for terminating a volunteer?

❏ Do these procedures include information needed to avoid charges of defamation?

❏ Do we have job-related medical information on volunteers?

> *Note: You may initially ask for certain physical or medical information as long as it is job-related. This is known as a bona fide occupational qualification. The burden is on your agency to show that physical requirements are necessary for the position. After the volunteer is "hired," additional physical or medical information may be required for health, safety, and emergency use.*

Orientation

Does our orientation for volunteers explain or include:

❏ Agency operations (including personnel policies)?

❏ Agency staffing and job functions?

❏ Safety procedures as they apply to--

    ❏ Working with clients?

    ❏ The program as a whole?

    ❏ Physical surroundings?

    ❏ Right to know information?

    ❏ Correction procedures?

        ❏ Professional assistance

        ❏ Self-assessment and correction

❏ Use of a personnel handbook that covers-

    ❏ Placement procedures?

    ❏ Our right to discharge volunteers?

❏ Explanation of Equal Employment Opportunity concerns as they affect working with the program and the people we serve?

❏ Duties of volunteer supervisors?

❏ Other written documentation?

Do we document orientation and training:

❏ By asking volunteers to sign a statement acknowledging their training?

❏ By standardizing our training in written form?

Training Program activity

Do we inform our volunteers about the following:

❏ That they are not to provide services for which they are unqualified, and which are not in their job description?

❏ That any volunteer is expected to use good judgment and caution in order to prevent accidents?

❏ How they are supervised?

❏ How they are reviewed and rewarded?

❏ How our organization handles complaints against volunteers?

❏ Policies and procedures related to data privacy and confidentiality?

(Note: For more information on this issue, see page 10.)

❏ Their access to training?

❏ Policies on sexual harassment?

What specific methods do we use to convey the above information?

❏ Individual tutoring

❏ Group training

❏ Print and audiovisual materials

❏ Other methods:

Note: The items listed above are not meant as a complete list of issues to address in hiring and training volunteers.

AUTOMOBILE LIABILITY

If your organization allows volunteers to drive as part of their duties, then be aware of the related risk and options for reducing that risk. The following questions will help you begin this process. Programs that are just developing risk management strategy may want to consider a continuum of actions to reduce automobile liability.

Agency-owned vehicles

Does our organization:

❏ Have insurance coverage that includes volunteer drivers?

❏ Inspect and maintain agency vehicles?

❏ Instruct volunteers in driving specific vehicles?

❏ Establish criteria for who drives vehicles?

Volunteer-owned vehicles

Included in this group are not only volunteers who drive as their primary responsibility, but also those who drive in the course of their work. This could include, for example, volunteers taking elderly people to appointments, or volunteers bringing groups of children to special events.

In all states, automobile liability insurance follows the automobile and in those states that have no-fault laws (Minnesota is a no-fault state) the coverage follows the individual's own policy. If a volunteer is driving his or her own vehicle, the primary policy in the event of the volunteer's own negligence, would be the volunteer's policy. If the organization has non-owned and hired-automobile liability insurance, it would be cover any excess over the limits of the primary policy.

The no-fault coverage follows the individual. In the event a passenger is injured, regardless of fault, the passenger would seek coverage from his or her own policy. In the case when injured persons do not have access to their own policy, the vehicle they are riding in would become the policy they would go to for coverage. If the operator of the vehicle they were riding in is the negligent driver, the passenger could bring suit against the driver if one of the following occur: *1)* medical expenses in excess of $4,000, *2)* disability, *3)* death or *4)*scarring.

Two other coverages might apply. In the event the passenger had no automobile liability insurance and the responsible party was uninsured, they could then use the volunteer's insurance to claim for underinsured or uninsured motorists coverage.

Does our organization have certificates of auto insurance on file?

❏ Are specific limits required?

❏ Is our organization listed as an additional insured? (In other words, is the organization also named on the volunteer's insurance policy?)

❏ Do our volunteers know they should provide notice to our organization if problems occur with their auto insurance?

❏ Do volunteers know that if there is a claim under their auto policy, their insurance should cover our organization?

❏ Can our organization assist with the cost of volunteers' auto insurance? Under what conditions?

❏ Does our organization need additional auto insurance?

- ❑ Does our organization keep up with vehicle inspection and maintenance schedules?
- ❑ Has our organization established criteria for when it's appropriate to use volunteers' vehicles?

Volunteers who drive as a part of their volunteer position

Does our organization:

- ❑ Check for appropriate drivers' icenses?
- ❑ Check driving records and compare them with an established organization standard?

Training provided to all drivers, regardless of vehicle use

Does our organization provide:

- ❑ Orientation to rules, procedures and expected behaviors, including safety rules for passengers while in the vehicle?
- ❑ Defensive driving courses and periodic retraining?
- ❑ Specialized vehicle training for volunteers operating vehicles for vulnerable people.

Other items

Does our organization:

- ❑ Have a system that monitors complaints about our drivers? (These systems protect the people your agency serves; they also establish an environment of safety for staff and volunteers.)
- ❑ Have a system for reporting injuries to the people we serve or damage to a vehicle?

DIRECTORS AND OFFICERS LIABILITY

Directors and officers liability insurance protects volunteer directors and officers against claims of wrongful acts. These claims may arise from members, employees, creditors, regulatory agencies, and the general public.

Essentially, this insurance covers the costs of a suit against a director or officer. These people must be sued in relation to their duties, and they must have acted in good faith.

The policy usually contains a two-part insuring agreement covering:

• Directors, officers, and trustees for wrongful acts committed during the scope of their duties.

• Your organization itself for amounts paid to directors, officers, and trustees to indemnify them for losses resulting from wrongful acts. To indemnify is to restore the victim of a loss, in whole or part, by payment, repair, or replacement.

As mentioned earlier, your organization could still be sued separately from individual directors or officers. If you want to protect against resulting defense costs or damages, then be sure to ask about *entity coverage*, which applies to the organization only.

Coverage applies to claims first made against the insureds and reported to the insurer during the policy period or the extended reporting period provided in the policy. (The *insureds* are the directors and officers covered under the policy.)

A directors and officers policy covers "wrongful acts" and generally does not apply to allegations of bodily injury or property damage. They pertain rather to assertions that acts, errors and omissions, breaches of fiduciary duties, misrepresentations or misstatements, producing economic rather than physical injury.

Again, this type of policy reimburses the organization for what it has paid to indemnify the insureds. This amount is specified by law, contract, or organization charter or by laws. The insurer may also pay directors, officers, or trustees directly for their personal losses, except where they have already been indemnified by the organization.

There are no standard forms for this type of insurance. Each insurance company offers its own form of coverage, exclusions, and conditions. Nonprofits may carry limits of $1 million, $5 million, or more. Consult an insurance agent or broker for recommendations on specific insurers, the policies they offer, their terms, and cost of coverage.

Some other questions to ask about this type of coverage follow:

❏ Does our organization have directors and officers liability insurance?

❏ If so, has the coverage been reviewed recently?

❏ What exclusions or riders are part of this coverage?

❏ What does this coverage cost?

❏ Do the benefits of this coverage outweigh the costs?

❏ What kind of coverage is needed, or what coverage do we want?

> ❏ Will the insurer defend the director or officer?
>
> ❏ Will the insurer pay damages?

❏ What options do we have for individuals to purchase this coverage?

❏ Purchase only when our organization identifies that it's needed?

> ❏ Add this coverage to individual's homeowners insurance?
>
> ❏ Purchase this coverage separately
>
> > ❏ At agency expense?
> >
> > ❏ At individual expense?

❏ Are our board members adequately informed about or trained in:

> ❏ Our operations?
>
> ❏ Our mission?
>
> ❏ Their roles and responsibilities?
>
> ❏ Their insurance options and considerations?

❏ Does our board periodically review programs and operations, including financial operations? (See other checklists in this section for related issues.)

❏ Do our board members have access to professional counsel (legal and financial)?

❏ Do we have clear procedures for indemnifying directors and officers?

> ❏ Our bylaws address this issue
>
> ❏ The provisions of the Minnesota Nonprofit Corporations Act (statute 317A.521) apply.

❏ If the policy contains an insured vs. insured exclusion, has it been deleted?

GENERAL LIABILITY

Bodily injury and property damage may result from icy sidewalks, loose carpets, or related hazards. These hazards can exist on your premises, or they can arise from your organization's operations. Liability for injuries and damages resulting from these hazards is insured under general liability insurance.

In reviewing your general liability coverage, begin with these questions:

❏ What general liability coverage do we have?

❏ Is this coverage reviewed and updated regularly?

❏ Are volunteers covered?

    ❏ They need to be covered for all their volunteer activity

    ❏ They need to be covered only for specific activities

❏ Do we regularly inspect buildings and land for safety? (For a general safety checklist, see page 63.)

❏ Do we post appropriate safety warnings? (Some of these may be required by law.)

❏ Do we offer safety training for volunteers?

    ❏ Is orientation for new volunteers similar to what we provide to employees?

    ❏ Do we offer periodic training on safety issues?

❏ Do we have a clear procedure for reporting general liability claims?

❏ Are procedures in writing, reviewed periodically, and provided to volunteers as part of their training?

❏ Do we have a system that monitors complaints related to general liability?

    ❏ Appropriate and convenient methods are available

    ❏ These methods create an environment that encourages accountability

❏ Does our organization use other locations, or alternative locations?

    ❏ If so, are these locations and staff members adequately covered for general liability?

❏ Do we have added general liability imposed by leases, contracts with funders, or other agreements?

❏ Do we hold special one-time events (such as fund raisers, receptions, or parties) that increase our general liability risk?

    ❏ If so, do we obtain liability coverage for these events?

❏ Do we need or want an umbrella policy for additional general liability protection? (An umbrella policy covers claims that exceed the limits offered by other policies.)

❏ Is personal injury covered (i.e. false arrest, slander, defamation of character)?

❏ Do we have coverage for liquor liability? (Or do we have a policy that liquor is not be served at events we sponsor?)

Note: Serving alcohol at functions presents potential problems with underaged drinking and drunk driving, your may be subject to host liquor liability. Obviously, the easiest way to deal with the problem is to serve only non-alcoholic beverages at an event. But if alcohol will be served, wristbands can help. You can set up a station to check identification and issue wristbands to those who are 21 and over. To encourage designated drivers, a different wrist band can be given to those people who promise not to drink. They can then receive free soda at the event. Be certain your liability insurance includes this coverage.

EXCESS LIABILITY

Many organizations elect to purchase higher limits of liability than are typically provided under the standard commercial general liability policy. These policies are written to provide protection against catastrophic liability losses. These policies are called excess policies or umbrellas. They take two forms, one is excess of loss and provides the same coverage at higher limits as the primary commercial general liability policy. The second is an umbrella and provides excess coverage over all liability of the organization including the automobile general liability and employers liability of the workers' compensation policy.

LIABILITY ASSOCIATED WITH VULNERABLE VOLUNTEERS

Some of your volunteers may be children or vulnerable adults. As mentioned in Part One of this handbook, vulnerable adults are those who–because of mental, physical, or emotional impairment–are unable or unlikely to report abuse or neglect. Note that this definition of vulnerable people is a flexible one. Some young adults are vulnerable, while many older adults are not.

Your policies and procedures must be designed to protect vulnerable people. Acknowledgments or releases from parents or guardians may be necessary for volunteers under a certain age. Also consider the liability implications of vulnerable people working with other vulnerable people. Problems could arise, for example, if elderly volunteers work with a child care program.

Involving vulnerable people as volunteers imposes a higher standard of care than usual. In addition, these programs may be regulated. For example, children may not be allowed to do certain activities because they violate curfew laws, or because the activity is hazardous.

As with other volunteers, the suggested approach is to treat vulnerable volunteers as regular employees for purposes of hiring, training, orienting, evaluating, or firing. For more help, see the checklist on personnel issues, page 40.

PROFESSIONAL OR MALPRACTICE LIABILITY

Your organization might be liable for the acts of any professional person or organization you employ or hire. Also, liability may arise from the acts of independent professionals on contract. This is called *contingent liability*.

The first step in managing these risks is carefully analyzing all services provided by or to your organization, looking for any that increase your risk of professional liability. Also ask your agent or broker which policies and limits of professional liability insurance are appropriate for your professional volunteers.

Verify professional licenses by checking with the appropriate licensing board in your state. You may want to obtain certificates of insurance from each of your professional volunteers.

One note on terminology as it relates to this coverage: Medical professionals include physicians, surgeons, dentists, psychologists, and people in other medical and health specialities. *Non-medical professionals* include accountants, lawyers, and people offering referral services, social services, and all other non-medical services.

It is possible that a volunteer covered by professional liability insurance may leave your organization. In that case, be sure to determine what, if any, liability your organization might face as a result. Talk to your agent, broker, or risk manager about any need to extend the coverage. This is especially important if the professional liability policy offered claims made coverage. Claims made coverage only applies to an injury or loss that is reported during the policy's period of coverage. In contrast, occurrence coverage provides protection for any injury or loss that occurred during the period covered by the policy regardless of when the claim is actually made.

Other questions to ask are these:

❏ Does our organization provide professional liability coverage for volunteers?

    ❏ If so, what is the extent of coverage?

    ❏ Are volunteers told about this coverage?

❏ Can our agency afford professional liability coverage?

❏ If our organization can't get or doesn't have professional liability coverage, can volunteers get this coverage?

    ❏ At agency expense?

    ❏ At volunteer expense?

❏ Do we try to coordinate our organization's professional liability coverage with the coverage our volunteers have?

❏ Does our agency review professional volunteer activity?

    ❏ By whom?

    ❏ How often?

    ❏ Do specific standards apply?

❏ Are professionals supervised?

    ❏ By staff?

    ❏ By other volunteers?

    ❏ By peers of volunteers?

❏ Does our organization have a system for filing and handling complaints against professional volunteers?

❏ Are professional volunteers truly volunteers?

    ❏ Could they possibly be construed as employees?

    ❏ Could they possibly be construed as independent contractors?

OFFERING SERVICES TO VULNERABLE PEOPLE

Here vulnerable people are the people you serve, not your volunteers. (There may be times when your organization serves vulnerable people and involves them as volunteers. In that case, also see page 46.)

Relevant questions to ask when your organization works with vulnerable people are these:

❏ Have we obtained copies of federal, state, and other laws and regulations that apply to vulnerable people?

    ❏ Have we determined how these affect our specific program?

    ❏ Have we determined other legal issues relating to work with vulnerable people?

❏ Has our board of directors issued a policy statement on working with vulnerable people and provided this policy to all volunteers?

❏ Have we received training on screening volunteers who will serve vulnerable people?

- ❏ Have we established standards or guidelines for screening volunteers?

    - ❏ Are we following these standards or guidelines?

    - ❏ Are we adequately trained to follow them?

- ❏ In establishing such screening, have we considered:

    - ❏ Criminal checks?

    - ❏ Psychological checks?

    - ❏ Descriptions of attitudes and behaviors?

    - ❏ References?

    - ❏ Driving records?

    - ❏ Job histories as they may relate to volunteer activity?

- ❏ Does our supervision of volunteers working with vulnerable people include:

    - ❏ Periodic contact?

    - ❏ Appraisal forms?

    - ❏ Required training?

    - ❏ Program evaluation?

    - ❏ Peer contact and supervision?

- ❏ Have we set standards for working with this population and communicated those standards to the volunteers, staff, and the people we serve?

- ❏ Do vulnerable people give us feedback on our services?

    - ❏ Do we have a systematic way of reviewing this feedback?

    - ❏ Do we have a system for handling complaints?

- ❏ Do we adequately train volunteers who could be considered professionals' delegates?

WORKERS COMPENSATION

In Minnesota, some state programs offer workers' compensation insurance for their volunteers. Some examples are the Department of Human Services, Civil Defense, the Department of Natural Resources, and county welfare boards. In many other cases, however, volunteers do not receive this protection.

Your organization might decide to provide protection for volunteers' work-related injuries and illness. Workers' compensation can be purchased on a "voluntary" basis to cover volunteer workers that are normally exempt from the Workers' Compensation law. As a practical matter, it can be difficult to obtain this coverage on a stand-alone basis or to add it to your existing policy. The state Assigned Risk Plan is a last resort for obtaining this coverage.

The voluntary compensation and employers liability coverage endorsement provides coverage for workers' compensation benefits of a given jurisdiction to employees who are not covered by the state workers' compensation law. In most states, workers' compensation benefit is considered the sole remedy. If the organization does not provide workers' compensation, it could be subject to legal action in the event of an on-the-job accident arising out of the employee's negligence. A part of the workers' compensation policy is coverage B. If the volunteer rejects the employer's offer and elects to bring suit, the Employer Liability coverage would respond.

A second option is to purchase a separate accident and health policy for the volunteers. This does not replace workers' compensation, but might reduce the possibility of the volunteer pursuing a legal recourse. A number of programs are available for this coverage.

In order to be sure you are pursuing the best course of action for your organization, you should consult with your agent or broker for the coverage best suited to your organization.

Some relevant questions to ask about this issue are:

❏ Have we checked our current workers' compensation coverage?

  Note: Governmental agencies may be covered by statute. Check to be sure.

❏ Have we assessed the benefits and costs of workers' compensation coverage against other means of insurance protection, including

    ❏ Agency accident or health insurance?

    ❏ Volunteers' own coverage?

❏ Do we coordinate coverage provided by volunteers with coverage provided by our agency?

❏ Do we routinely encourage safety procedures, including:

    ❏ Conducting periodic insurance reviews for our entire organization?

    ❏ Providing orientations that keep volunteers aware of safety issues?

❏ Have safety standards been developed for job descriptions?

❏ Are volunteers checked for physical restrictions that would jeopardize ability to perform work?

❏ Has a safety and training program been established?

OTHER ISSUES THAT CAN AFFECT YOUR VOLUNTEER PROGRAMS

The preceding pages outlined issues relating to seven areas of risk your organization may face. However, there are other types of risk to consider, including those listed below.

Accounts receivable

Accounts receivable are records of money due to your organization. Potential loss in this area includes:

• The cost of new books (records)

• Recollecting and reconstructing information

• Inability to collect accounts receivable due to loss of information

Buildings

Questions to answer about your organization's buildings include:

Are they leased or owned?

• If owned, who covers the maintenance, tax, and rental expenses?

- Who is responsible for improvements?

- Who is responsible for heating damage (for example, to plate glass)?

Contents

Contents is an insurance term that includes furniture, fixtures, equipment, and supplies. Relevant questions about contents include:

- Is there a budget for replacement, loss, and depreciation of contents?

- Do we have current lists of all contents?

- Do our contents include leased or borrowed property?

Note: Computers may be separately insured to include the cost of reconstructing and re-entering data.

Extra expenses

Extra expenses are those needed to continue operations and services following a fire or other property loss. These expenses include:

- Rental of temporary premises and equipment

- Replacement of equipment

- Moving expense

- Utilities

Key person insurance

Key person insurance is taken out and paid for by your agency. If a key person in your organization dies, this insurance covers the expense of temporary help and of searching for a replacement.

Valuable papers

Valuable papers include financial and statistical records, case histories, deeds, mortgages, historical documents, and computer disks. To protect these papers, keep inventories of them and store copies of these papers outside your premises. Also consider keeping some originals off your premises, perhaps in a safe deposit box.

Fiduciary liability

This area of risk concerns your organization's benefit programs, including those that relate to the Employee Retirement Income Security Act (ERISA), pensions, medical insurance, life insurance, and dental benefits. When considering this area ask:

- Do we have lists of appropriate benefit programs to track?

- Who administers these programs?

- Who audits these programs?

- Who is responsible for seeing that the programs comply with regulations?

Volunteers Insurance

Some organizations provide the following for their volunteers:

- Accident insurance - modest limits of excess coverage

- Medical

- Accidental death and dismemberment

- Excess personal liability

- Excess automobile liability

There are a number of comparable insurance programs available, and you should consult your insurance agent or company to obtain detailed information.

Employee Dishonesty and Money & Securities

This area of concern relates to the appropriate controls for audit procedures, and controls to minimize the potential losses caused by embezzlement and the loss of money or securities both at the premises and away from the premises. Things to consider:

- Are the appropriate audit controls established and are they being followed?

- Are there limitations on the period of time an individual can remain in a position?

- If you handle cash, checks or securities, are they deposited immediately?

- Do the premises have security?

- Is the safe fire-resistive?

- Are two signatures required for checks over a certain amount?

- Are responsibilities split so no one person controls the entire process - registering deposits, withdrawals, and balancing the accounts?

SUMMARY OF PART FIVE

Every organization that involves volunteers faces different legal risks. Yet certain kinds of risks are fairly common across organizations. These include:

- **Personnel issues**

- **Automobile liability**

- **Directors and officers liability**

- **General liability**

- **Liability associated with vulnerable volunteers**

- **Professional and malpractice liability**

- **Offering services to vulnerable people**

- **Workers compensation**

- **Volunteers' Insurance**

- **Employee dishonesty and money & securities**

APPENDIX:

Other Useful Forms and Checklists

RISK MANAGEMENT WORKSHEET

Use the following worksheet to think through each step of the risk management process. Make multiple copies of this worksheet, and fill out one copy for each specific risk you identify.

Step I: Identify the risk

General type of risk

Automobile liability, professional liability, directors' and officers' liability, workers' compensation, general liability, employee dishonesty, computer coverage or other:

Specific risk

Naming the specific risk is especially important if the general risk falls under professional liability or "other." (For example, loss of accounts receivable is a specific risk that falls under the category of "other.") This step is also crucial if your organization serves vulnerable people, or if any of your volunteers are vulnerable people.

Step 2: Measure the risk

Loss potential

For liability loss, include the cost of claim defense and settlement. For property loss, include the replacement cost. Also include the best estimate for the loss that will cause an interruption to your business. The increased cost of rent, expediting expense to get back in business, and any business interruption loss cause by loss of your facility. Consult your agent, broker, or insurer for help.

Minnesota Office of Citizenship and Volunteer Services
Planning it Safe: How to Control Liability & Risk in Volunteer Programs

As you are reviewing the loss potential, it is a good time to start thinking about your contingency plan. What do you do if a loss occurs. Most businesses that do not have a contingency plan never get back into business.

Step 3: Select methods to control or finance the risk and implement them

Available methods to control the risk

Can the risk be avoided or eliminated? How?

Can the risk be reduced? How? (For example, by more carefully selecting and training employees and volunteers.)

Can the risk be transferred to others? (For example, by arranging for another organization to perform professional services.)

Available methods to finance the risk

Can the loss be retained (assumed)?

Can part of the loss be retained?

Can the loss be insured?

Cost of that insurance:

Methods selected to control and finance the risk

For effective risk management, always select at least one control method and one finance method for each risk.

Methods of control:

Retention/Deductible:

Insurance selected:

Actions needed to Implement these methods:

Interview several insurance agents and/or companies to find out who best understands your business. Ask for a list of references of similar types of risks or nonprofit experience.

Get competitive quotes from two agents. Don't involve too many agents as there are only so many insurance companies seeking nonprofit business.

Look at the cost vs. benefit of each proposal. Assume as much risk as you have a tolerance for through the use of deductibles or risk minimization or elimination. Protect against the catastrophe; don't swap dollars with an insurance company.

Get competitive bids every 3 to 5 years, don't shop every year, as it is better to establish long term relationships with your insurance agent and company.

Require an annual review with your agent or company to assess your experience, new coverages, changes in your business and update your risks and their loss potential as the environment you work in does change.

Minnesota Office of Citizenship and Volunteer Services
Planning it Safe: How to Control Liability & Risk in Volunteer Programs

Step 4: Manage claims and losses

Do we have a system for reporting this claim or loss? (Describe it briefly here.)

Do we have a system for settling this claim or loss? (Describe it briefly here.)

How will we keep records of this claim or loss?

Do you have your insurance agent and company keep you apprised of large claims and the possible impact they could have on your business; both financial and in media relations?

Have you established who will be a spokesperson to the media? Have all inquires, written and oral, referred to that person.

Step 5: Monitor the risk management program and make necessary changes

Describe the effectiveness of the risk control methods:

Describe the effectiveness of retaining or insuring this risk:

Recommend any necessary changes:

Cost of these changes:

Forms

RECORD OF ACCIDENT/INJURY/PROPERTY DAMAGE

Use this form to record all accidents, injuries, and losses to property. This information is needed to report claims and losses to your insurers. Your agent, broker, or insurer may ask you to complete additional forms.

Make a separate report for each person. Attach additional sheets if you need more space.

Name of organization: _____

Address: _____

Accident location: _____

        On premises?   ☐ Yes ☐ No

Date of occurrence: _____

Time of occurrence: _____ AM/PM _____

Date reported: _____

Reported to: _____

Injured person(s) _____

        Name: _____

        Telephone: _____

        Address: _____

        Occupation: _____

        Employer: _____

Object or equipment causing the accident: _____

Person controlling the object or equipment: _____

Describe property lost or damaged: _____

_____

_____

      Estimated cost: _____

      Actual cost::_____

      Nature of loss or damage: _____

      Object/equipment/substance causing loss: _____

_____

Describe how the accident/injury/property damage occurred:_____

_____

_____

Did injured person leave work?   ☐ Yes ☐ No

Eexpected date of return to work: _____

Did injured person go to doctor?   ☐ Yes ☐ No

Physician's name: _____

Did injured person go to hospital? ☐ Yes ☐ No

Name of hospital:_____

Witnesses?_____

_____

What alleged act, failure to act or condition, in your opinion, directly contrib-uted to the injury or property damage?

_____

_____

Were there police reports?_____

Were emergency medical services provided?_____

Action taken or planned to prevent recurrence of loss:_____

Checklist

POLICY ORDER OR RENEWAL

Insurance policies offer coverage for specific term—that is, a specific period of time. To continue coverage after the term expires, the insurer must renew the policy.

Effective risk management includes reviewing the performance of the insurer and the policy before the renewal date. You might decide to ask for changes in coverage, or even seek a new insurer. In addition, your present insurer may offer some changes in coverage or premium. This means that managing policy renewals is essential.

Following are some relevant items to consider before renewing any insurance policy.

1. Type of risk

2. Actual losses:

3. Estimated loss potential:

4. Agent or broker (currently servicing risk or to be consulted on risk):

5. Date of interview with agent:

6. Interview comments:

7. Action planned:

8. Is this insurance generally available from many or just a few insurers?

9. Insurance company proposed:

10. Insurance recommended by agent:

11. Agent's comments on insurer (insurer's financial condition and service record):

12. Application completed (type of application and completion date):

13. Can coverage be bound?

14. Binder received from agent:

15. Insurance effective date:

16. Expected date of policy delivery:

17. Actual date of policy delivery:

18. Policy explained by agent:

    a. scope of coverage:

    b. exclusions:

    c. major conditions:

    d. policyholder duties:

    e. claims to be reported to:

19. How much time will agent need to prepare for the renewal?

Minnesota Office of Citizenship and Volunteer Services
Planning it Safe: How to Control Liability & Risk in Volunteer Programs

Checklist

SAFETY AND SECURITY

Use this checklist as a way to start assessing the safety and security of your organization. After reviewing the checklist results, you can decide which safety issues need further attention in your risk management program.

First Aid

First aid supplies are maintained	☐ Yes	☐ No
Emergency phone numbers posted		
Fire Department	☐ Yes	☐ No
Doctor	☐ Yes	☐ No-
Hospital	☐ Yes	☐ No
Employees/volunteers trained in first aid procedures	☐ Yes	☐ No
Employees/volunteers trained in CPR procedures	☐ Yes	☐ No
First aid supplies and procedures are checked monthly	☐ Yes	☐ No

Medical facilities

Physician or clinic designated for referral of injuries	☐ Yes	☐ No
Physician familiar with volunteer organization's operations	☐ Yes	☐ No

Safety review

Key operational and product hazards identified		
Before accident	☐ Yes	☐ No
After accident	☐ Yes	☐ No
Organization has standards for purchase of safe equipment and supplies`	☐ Yes	☐ No
Safety and security review of new facilities and operations	☐ Yes	☐ No
Procedure for compliance with government regulatory requirement	☐ Yes	☐ No

Disaster emergencies

Written plan for emergency action and recovery

Fire and explosion	☐ Yes	☐ No
Tornado and flood	☐ Yes	☐ No

Shutdown procedure ☐ Yes ☐ No

Evacuation procedure ☐ Yes ☐ No

Recovery plan ☐ Yes ☐ No

Provisions for:

Copies of vital records ☐ Yes ☐ No

Temporary premises ☐ Yes ☐ No

Temporary equipment ☐ Yes ☐ No

Restoration of employee and volunteer services ☐ Yes ☐ No

Inspection of premises

Lighting is adequate, including stairways ☐ Yes ☐ No

Emergency lighting needed ☐ Yes ☐ No

Overloaded electrical circuits ☐ Yes ☐ No

Use of extension cords forbidden ☐ Yes ☐ No

Handrails on stairs in good repair ☐ Yes ☐ No

Loose treads on stairways ☐ Yes ☐ No

Loose carpets or tiles on floors ☐ Yes ☐ No

Adequate space between gas and electric equipment and combustibles ☐ Yes ☐ No

Combustibles stored under stairs or in concealed space ☐ Yes ☐ No

Smoking forbidden or restricted ☐ Yes ☐ No

Trash is removed daily ☐ Yes ☐ No

Minnesota Office of Citizenship and Volunteer Services
Planning it Safe: How to Control Liability & Risk in Volunteer Programs

Fire extinguishers

        Located throughout premises, including kitchen   ☐ Yes   ☐ No

        Maintained in good condition   ☐ Yes   ☐ No

        Personnel trained in proper use   ☐ Yes   ☐ No

Employees trained in fire procedures   ☐ Yes   ☐ No

Restrooms kept safe and sanitary   ☐ Yes   ☐ No

Crime

Employee references checked   ☐ Yes   ☐ No

Bank and other accounts reconciled by person who does not handle receipts and disbursements   ☐ Yes   ☐ No

Bank deposits made regularly at varied times   ☐ Yes   ☐ No

Cash control system established and followed   ☐ Yes   ☐ No

Cash on premises kept to minimum   ☐ Yes   ☐ No

Employees trained to report suspicious persons   ☐ Yes   ☐ No

Doors, side and rear, kept locked   ☐ Yes   ☐ No

Automobile

Driver selection

Motor Vehicle Records (MVRS) ordered on all personnel who drive on organization business   ☐ Yes   ☐ No

Persons with frequency of accidents and/or violations not allowed to drive for organization   ☐ Yes   ☐ No

Written driving rules circulated   ☐ Yes   ☐ No

Accident review

Organization reviews all accidents   ☐ Yes   ☐ No

Date of Inspection:

Inspected by: _____

Report sent to: _____

Date of follow-up inspection: _____

GUIDELINES FOR EXTENDING LIABILITY PROTECTION TO VOLUNTEER DRIVERS

Policy: It is a requirement that all volunteers complete a Volunteer Driver Authorization Form and be approved to drive before driving any vehicle on agency business. The form describes the purpose for using the vehicle and if approved, confirms an agency relationship between the driver and the organization. The authorization results in liability protection for volunteers while driving in the course and scope of their assigned duties.

Driver Authorization Criteria

All sections of the authorization must be completed. Incomplete forms will be returned for completion.

Violation and/or accidents - Rejection will be automatic if any one or combination of the following exist:

- Moving violation(s) and/or at fault accident(s) within the past 3 years:
    Two or more incidents
    Six or more points

- Violations within the past 12 months for:
    Drunken Driving
    Driving Under the Influence of Drugs
    Reckless Driving

- Driver Experience - Rejection will be automatic when someone has:
    Had their reinstated license in effect less than one year after revocation.
    Had their license less than two years. (They do not have enough on-the-road experience to be driving agency vehicles.)

- Anyone required to drive a 12-15 passenger van must also meet the following guidelines
    Be al least 18 years of age.
    Must have completed a qualified van driver training program consisting of at least 4 hours of classroom and behind-the-wheel training.

- Purpose for using the vehicle is another basis for determining approval or rejection.
    Some examples of approved usage are:
      Field trips for educational purposes and have on-site supervision
      Educational programs which require training outside the area.
      Business errands
      Conferences, meetings and events

    Some examples of denial are:
      Field trips that do not have approval.

If a volunteer has an out-of-state license, they must attach a notarized statement listing any moving violations and describing any accidents they have been involved in for the past three years. This applies to drivers with many years experience who have a Minnesota license for less than three years.

If authorization is approved notice will be provided to the individual.

If authorization is rejected an memo will be sent explaining why.

Form

MINNESOTA DEPARTMENT OF PUBLIC SAFETY

BUREAU OF CRIMINAL APPREHENSION

CRIMINAL JUSTICE INFORMATION SYSTEMS

1246 UNIVERSITY AVENUE ST. PAUL, MINNESOTA 55104

612-642-0670

Criminal History Record Information maintained by this agency is classified as Private Data. Minnesota State Statutes 13.05, Subdivision 4, requires that the subject of Private Data give his or her informed consent prior to dissemination of this data to any person or agency. Paragraph (d) of this statute states in part that:

"Informed consent shall not be deemed to have been given an individual subject of data by the signing of any statement authorizing any person or agency to disclose information about him or her unless the statement is:

1. In plain language;

2. Dated;

3. Specific in designating the particular persons or agencies the data subject is authorizing to disclose information about him or her;

4. Specific as to the nature of the information he or she is authorizing to be disclosed;

5. Specific as to the persons or agencies to whom he or she is authorizing information to be disclosed

6. Specific as to the purposes for which the information may be used by any of the parties named in clause 5, both at the time of the disclosure and at any time in the future;

7. Specific as to its expiration date, which should be within a reasonable period of time, not to exceed one year except in the case of authorizations given in connection with applications for life insurance or noncancelable or guaranteed renewable health insurance and identified as such, two years after the date of the policy.

This agency further requires that the informed consent be notarized to insure the validity of the signature. Also, in order to conduct a search of our files, we must have the subject's Full Name and Date of Birth.

In addition, a $8.00 charge for processing this request will be assessed. The $8.00 can be in the form of a money order, cashier's check or business check. Personal checks are not acceptable; and cash should not be sent by mail. A self-addressed, stamped envelope must be included for a return reply.

If you have any questions regarding the above-outlined procedures, or if you require any assistance, please contact the Bureau of Criminal Apprehension; Criminal Justice Information Systems Section.

Company Name
Street Address
City, State and Zip
Phone
Date

The following named individual has made application with this agency for _____

_____

Last Name of Applicant (please print): _____

First Name (please print): _____

Middle (full) (please print): _____

Maiden, Alias or Former (please print): _____

Date of Birth: _____   Sex (M or F): _____

Social Security Number: _____

I authorize the Minnesota Bureau of Criminal Apprehension to disclose all criminal history record information to

_____ for the purpose of

_____ as

_____ with this agency.

The expiration of this authorization shall be for no longer than one year from the date of my signature.

_____   _____
        Signature of Applicant   Date

Forms

CHILD PROTECTION BACKGROUND CHECK ACT SAMPLE FORM

Organization/agency/school district
Address
Phone number

Because the position for which you are applying will require to provide care, treatment, education, training, instruction, or recreation to children, the _____ will request the Bureau of Criminal Apprehension (BCA) to perform a background check on you under Minnesota Statutes Chapter 299C.62.

Have you ever been convicted of any of the following crimes? (If yes, please attach a description of the crime and the particulars of the conviction).   ☐ Yes   ☐ No

BACKGROUND CHECK CRIMES

Under Minnesota Statutes Chapter 299C

☐ Murder   ☐ Manslaughter

☐ Kidnapping   ☐ Arson

☐ Criminal Sexual Conduct   ☐ Prostitution Related Crime

☐ Any Assault Crime Against a Minor   ☐ Felony Level Assault

☐ Any of the following Child Abuse Crimes committed against Minor victims, constituting a violation of Minnesota Statutes Sections:

609.185,(5)	Murder in the 1st Degree
609.221	Assault in the 1st Degree
609.222	Assault in the 2nd Degree
609.223	Assault in the 3rd Degree
609.224	Assault in the 4th Degree
609.322	Solicitation, Inducement and Promotion of Prostitution
609.323	Receiving Profit Derived from Prostitution
609.324	Other prohibited acts of Prostitution
609.342	Criminal Sexual Conduct in the 1st Degree
609.343	Criminal Sexual Conduct in the 2nd Degree
609.344	Criminal Sexual Conduct in the 3rd Degree
609.345	Criminal Sexual Conduct in the 4th Degree
609.352	Solicitation of Children to Engage in Sexual Conduct
609.377	Malicious Punishment of a Child
609.378	Neglect or Endangerment of a Child
152.021, subd. 1,(4)	Controlled Substance Crime in the 1st Degree
152.022, subd. 1,(5)	Controlled Substance Crime in the 2nd Degree
152.022, subd. 1,(6)	Controlled Substance Crime in the 2nd Degree

152.023, subd. 1,(3)	Controlled Substance Crime in the 3rd Degree
152.023, subd. 1,(4)	Controlled Substance Crime in the 3rd Degree
152.023, subd. 1,(6)	Controlled Substance Crime in the 3rd Degree
152.023, subd. 1,(7)	Controlled Substance Crime in the 3rd Degree
152.024, subd. 1,(2)	Controlled Substance Crime in the 4th Degree
152.024, subd. 1,(3)	Controlled Substance Crime in the 4th Degree
152.024, subd. 1,(4)	Controlled Substance Crime in the 4th Degree

As the subject of a _____ (type of employment) background check, your rights include:

• to be informed that _____ (your agency) will request this check for becoming or continuing as an employee or volunteer, and to determine whether you have been convicted of any of the above specified crimes, and

• to be informed of BCA's response and obtain a copy of the report, and

• to challenge the accuracy and completeness of any information contained in the report, and

• to be informed whether _____ (your agency) has denied your application because of the BCA's response and not to be required directly or indirectly to pay the cost of the background check.

Minnesota statutes and the BCA require you to complete the following information in order to complete the background check:

Last Name of Applicant (please print): _____

First Name (please print): _____

Middle (full) (please print): _____

Maiden, Alias or Former (please print): _____

Date of Birth: _____   Sex (M or F): _____

Social Security Number: _____

_____   _____
           Signature of Applicant   Date

WAIVER FORMS

The following examples of waivers are taken from Minnesota cases. Please remember that courts will carefully review waivers and often courts will refuse to enforce the waivers. The two waivers below were enforced, but even the same waiver may not be enforced for a different kind of activity.

- I, [INSERT INDIVIDUAL'S NAME], the undersigned, while engaging in [INSERT DESCRIPTION OF ACTIVITY], do hereby agree for myself, my heirs, executors, administrators and assigns, that neither said [INSERT NAME OF ORGANIZATION] nor any of its officers, directors, employees, agents, members or volunteers shall be held responsible or liable for any negligence, or personal injury, or death, or property loss, or damage suffered or sustained by me in connection with or arising out of or resulting from any or all [INSERT ACTIVITY] engaged in by me; and further, I do hereby, for myself, my heirs, administrators, executors, and assigns, assume all risk whatsoever of personal injury or death or property damage or loss in connection with or arising out of or resulting from any or all [INSERT ACTIVITY] engaged in by me, and absolve and release said [INSERT NAME OF ORGANIZATION], its officers, directors, employees, agents, members or volunteers, of and from all liability thereof, and further, I do hereby covenant and agree for myself, my heirs, executors, administrators, and assigns, not to sue, arrest, attach, or prosecute said [INSERT NAME OF ORGANIZATION], its officers, directors, employees, agents, members or volunteers for or on account of any such personal injury or death or property damage or loss, it being my express intent and purpose to bind myself, my heirs, executors, administrators, and assigns hereby."

Malecha v. St. Croix Valley Skydiving Club, Inc., 392 N.W.2d 727 (Minn. App. 1986) (waiver for skydiving school).

- It is expressly agreed that [DESCRIBE TYPE OF ACTIVITY] shall be undertaken by the undersigned at the undersigned's sole risk and that [INSERT NAME OF ORGANIZATION] and its directors, officers, employees, agents, members or volunteers shall not be liable for any claims, demands, injuries, damages, actions or causes of action, whatsoever to the undersigned or property arising out of or connected with the negligence of [INSERT NAME OF ORGANIZATION] or the negligence of its directors, officers, employees, agents, members or volunteers, and the undersigned does hereby expressly forever release and discharge [INSERT NAME OF ORGANIZATION] and its directors, officers, employees, agents, members or volunteers from all such claims, demands, injuries, damages, actions or causes of action, and from all acts of active or passive negligence on the part of [INSERT NAME OF ORGANIZATION] and its directors, officers, employees, agents, members or volunteers."

Schlobohm v. Spa Petite, Inc., 326 N.W.2d 920 (Minn. 1982) (waiver for health club).

WHERE TO FIND MORE INFORMATION

Statutes and regulations that apply to volunteers

Note: The following are references to Minnesota Statutes (1997)

3.736	Minnesota State Tort Claims Act
3.739	Court Referred Volunteers
13	Minnesota Government Data Practices Act
245	Human Services Licensing
317A	Minnesota Nonprofit Corporation Act
466	Tort Liability, Political Subdivisions (Tort Claims Act for local governments other than state government)
604.02	Contributory Negligence
604A.01	Good Samaritan Law
604A.10	Liability of Food Donors
604A.11	Voluntary Athletic and Officials
604A.12	Livestock Activities
626.556	Required reporting for abuse of minors
626.557	Required reporting for abuse of vulnerable adults

Department of Human Services Regulation 9543.3030 requires background checks for Chapter 245 facilities such as group homes and day care providers.

Other materials on legal issues relating to volunteers

The following books, periodicals, and articles provide more in-depth information on the topics discussed in this handbook. Most of the materials listed are available to Minnesota residents through the resource collection at the Minnesota Office on Citizenship and Volunteer Services (MOCVS), Department of Administration, 117 University Avenue, St. Paul, MN, 55155, 612-296-4731 or 1-800-652--9747. Some of the materials may also be available through public libraries, law libraries, volunteer centers, and state offices on volunteerism.

Am I Covered for... ?, Second Edition, Terry S. Chapman, Mary L. Lai, and Elmer L. Steinbock, Nonprofit Risk Management Center

Discusses various types of insurance coverage and shows volunteers how they can protect themselves (283 pp).

Answers to Volunteers' Liability and Insurance Questions, Nonprofit Risk Management Center (1991).

Provides basic information about legal and insurance matters affecting volunteers (14 pp).

Big Brothers/Big Sisters; A Study of Volunteer Recruitment and Screening, Phoebe A. Roaf, Joseph P. Tierney, and Dianista E. I. Hunte, Public/Private Ventures

Final report of study on methods to attract volunteers, especially members of minorities, and which methods deter potential volunteers (48 pp).

Board Liability-Guide for Nonprofits Directors, Daniel L. Kurtz, Moyer Bell Ltd. (1988).

Contains an in-depth examination of legal responsibilities of directors. These include how to avoid and manage conflicts of interest, the business judgment rule, why directors get sued, statutory liabilities and how indemnification works, need for insurance, gaps in directors and officers coverage, case studies for the "real world," and more. Examples illustrate the operational implications of duties (196 pp).

Charity is No Defense: The Impact of the Insurance Crisis on Nonprofit Organizations and an Examination of Alternative Insurance Mechanisms, 22 U.S. F. Law Review 599, (1988).

Includes a good, thorough discussion of alternative insurance methods in the nonprofit context.

"Checklist for Boards", National information Center on Volunteerism, adapted from **The Board Member. Decision Maker for the Non-Profit Organization** (1977).

Consists of a four-page checklist for unpaid volunteer members of boards of nonprofit organizations.

Compensation for Harm from Charitable Activity, Charles Tremper, 76 Cornell Law Review 401 (1991).

Contains an overview of the charitable sector. This is a good critique of tort law as it applies to nonprofit organizations. It also contains a discussion of the insurance crisis in the context of nonprofit organizations. This book helps in understanding the general issues.

D and 0: Yes or No?: Directors and Officers Insurance for the Volunteer Board, Nonprofit Risk Management Center (1991).

Designed to address the concerns of volunteer directors and officers of nonprofit organizations (20 pp).

From the Top Down: The Executive Role in Volunteer Program Success, Revised Edition, Susan J. Ellis, Energize Associates (1996).

Written for top-level executives of agencies that already work with or plan to involve volunteers. Emphasizing vision and commitment, it suggests salaried staff should be treated as volunteers by asking executives to offer traditional volunteer motivators: choice, positive working environment, and recognition to both paid and unpaid staff. This book includes special sections on legal and accounting issues (210 pp).

"Guide to Insurance for Volunteers," Maureen Aspin and Steve McCurley, Voluntary Action Leadership, Fall 1977, pp 16-17.

Summarizes the types of insurance available for volunteers. This article identifies questions to ask in investigating appropriate insurance protection and providing coverage for volunteers (2 pp).

Insurance Coverage for Volunteers, Minnesota Office on Volunteer Services (1984).

Provides an overview of concerns related to insurance for volunteers and defines insurance terms; includes a bibliography (8 pp).

Insurance Legal Liability for Volunteers, The National VOLUNTEER Center (1990).

Contains information on insurance coverage for volunteers, including types of coverage available, methods for obtaining coverage, and what to look for in liability insurance policies (13 pp).

Insurance for Volunteers and Voluntary Organizations, Stan Pope and Wanda Bielak, VOLUNTEER-The National Center (1983).

Discusses, in brief, general terms, volunteers and general liability, accident and disability coverage, and automobile insurance. Examines issues and coverage available both for agencies and individual volunteers (15 pp).

Insurance Information for Volunteer Sponsoring Units, Organizations and the Individual Volunteer, Minnesota Insurance Information Center (1976).

Discusses some of the risk problems of volunteers and sponsoring organizations, as well as how insurance meets certain needs (6 pp).

The Law of Tax-Exempt Organizations, Sixth Edition, Bruce Hopkins, John Wiley and Sons (1996).

Gives an extensive explanation of the history and rationale for offering tax exemption to nonprofit organizations. This is one of the leading sources of information on federal tax-exemption for nonprofit corporations. It explains in-depth the various types of nonprofit organizations and the tax considerations and regulations for each. Written in nontechnical language, it can be understood even by a volunteer on a board of directors who is new to this area of law. The book is supplemented yearly (949 pp).

A Legal Handbook for Nonprofit Corporation Volunteers or What to Do Till the Lawyer Comes, On-Line Edition, James D. DeWitt, 1997. http://www2.polarnet.com/~jdewitt/vlh

This manual is intended for all volunteer managers, members of the board of dietors, and officers of nonprofit corporations. Includes a short course on legal issues, discussion of risk management and how to start a nonprofit organization.

Legal Issues for Service-Learning Programs: A Community Service Brief, Anna Seidman and Charles Tremper, Nonprofit Risk Management Center, Washington, D.C., 1994

Provides general guidance on legal liability, negligence, insurance, and risk management; suggests strategies to prevent legal problems; offers suggestions for adhering to pertinent laws and regulations.

Legal Issues: A NCSL Resource Package, ACTION/National Center for Service-Learning (1978).

One of a series of resource collections developed by the National Center for Service-Learning, this source provides information on topics of interest to student volunteers, coordinators, school administrators and staff who work with student volunteers. The packet include articles, forms, and other materials relating to volunteer liability and insurance concerns (144 pp).

Legal Issues: Resource Booklet, ACTION/National Center for Service Learning (n.d.).

Summarizes the legal implications, responsibilities, and liabilities involved in settings where students are both learners and workers. Sets out general steps to be taken to gain the maximum feasible protection consistent with the educational and social purpose of the program. Aimed at service-learning educators, administrators, and practitioners (22 pp).

"Legal Issues for Liabilities and Responsibilities of Board Members of Nonprofit Corporations," Steve McCurley, Minnesota Office on Volunteer Services Newsletter, Volume 3, Number 5, Sept.-Oct. 1978, pp 4-5.

Offers a brief description of the duties and potential liability of the members of a board of directors for a nonprofit organization (2 pp).

Liability in Correctional Volunteer Programs, Planning for Potential Problems, Peter J. Gurfein, ABA National Volunteer Parole Aide Program (1975).

Presents basic information that state agencies and volunteer organizations need to understand the legal implications of participating in the correctional system (45 pp).

Liability Insurance and the Volunteer Driver. An Analysis of the Impact of Insurance Availability and Cost on Minnesota Volunteer Drivers and Volunteer Transportation Programs, Minnesota Department of Transportation (1990).

Reports on a survey of volunteers and managers on the effect of volunteer driving on liability insurance. Presents three recommendations for addressing the problems of car liability insurance (121 pp).

Liability Insurance Purchasing, Charles Tremper, Support Centers of America (1990).

Provides a nuts-and-bolts guide to liability insurance. This publication explains the insurance process in lay terms and offers practical suggestions for assessing an organization's insurance needs and obtaining coverage. Based on a series of articles originally published in the NonProfit Times (8 pp).

The Nonprofit Board's Role in Risk Management: More Than Buying Insurance, Charles Tremper and George Babcock, The National Center for Nonprofit Boards (1990).

Presents a concise guide to fulfilling the board's risk management respons-bilities. The central thesis of the booklet is that the board's responsibility extends beyond protecting itself from liability to encompass all risks in the organization's functions. This publication presents a systematic procedure for the board to use in discharging this obligation (20 pp).

Nonprofit Corporations, Organizations, and Associations, Howard Oleck, Prentice Hall Inc. (1988).

Considered a treatise on nonprofit law, this book is the most comprehensive authority on the subject, covering everything from tax considerations to management concerns and start-up. The book devotes an entire chapter to litigation in the nonprofit context. That chapter is a practical guide of sorts, since it also includes model litigation forms; it also discusses indemnifica-tion. This book is supplemented occasionally as new issues are raised. (1251 pp).

Nonprofit Litigation: A Practical Guide with Forms and Checklists, Steve Bachman, Esq., John Wiley and Sons, Inc. (1992).

Provides nuts-and-bolts information needed to understand all side of nonprofit litigation. This publication allows directors and executives of nonprofit agen-cies to work more effectively and efficiently with attorneys. It covers such topics as structuring a nonprofit, controlling the costs of litigation, and litigation strategies (400 pp).

The Nonprofit Organization Handbook, Second Edition, Trace D. Connors, McGraw Hill.

Discusses management and planning for nonprofit organizations. Six main topics are included: organization and corporate principles; leadership, management, and control; human resources management; sources of revenue; public relations and communications; financial management and administration (740 pp).

Nonprofit Organizations: Rights and Liabilities for Members, Directors, and Officers, Elaine Hadden, Callaghan (1987).

Offers a quick overview of nonprofit corporation acts in other states, as well as an understandable explanation of the difference between members, directors, and officers. This book also contains helpful information on the relationship between directors and officers and staff of an organization. (148 pp).

No Surprises: Controlling Risks in Volunteer Programs, Charles Tremper and Gwyne Kostin, Nonprofit Risk Management Center.

Suggests ways to prevent injuries, such as screening staff, members and volunteers. As well as ways to prevent mismanagement and other types of damage (60 pp).

Opportunity or Dilemma: Court-Referred Community Service Workers, Katherine H. Noyes, Virginia Department of Volunteerism (1990 revised edition).

Explores the trend of court-ordered community service as it affects community agencies and their volunteer programs. The contents are based on research and include general information, specific how-to-do-it material, and key resources (119 pp).

Organizations' Liability for Torts of Volunteers, Jeffrey Kahn, 133 University of Pennsylvania Law Review 1433 (1985).

Focuses on how tort law affects volunteers. This article gives an excellent overview of tort law concepts and a well-rounded discussion of abolishing charitable immunity. It is helpful for understanding the role of the volunteer in the issue of liability.

Primer on Insurance for Volunteers, Richard Williams, Korda Project (n.d.).

Discusses three primary areas of insurance that often concern volunteers, along with sources of insurance coverage. The three areas covered are accident insurance, personal liability, and automobile liability insurance (17 pp).

Risk Management and Insurance for Nonprofit Managers, Byron Stone and Carol North, First Non Profit Risk Pooling Trust (1988).

Provides a thorough guide to risk management for nonprofits. This publication presents risk management as an integral part of managing a nonprofit organization. Designed for hands-on use, this over-sized paperback provides numerous forms and checklists to guide novice and expert alike through the phases of risk management. Included is a glossary of insurance terms (157 pp).

Risk Management for Smart Communities, (n.d.) a series of materials available from Southern Rural Development Center, P.O, Box 5446, Mississippi State, MS 39762:

> **Risk Management Manual** explains the risk management process in simple language and examines 12 common exposure areas.

> **Risk Management Workbook** contains checklists, sample letters and memos, worksheets, and other tools to start a risk management program.

> **Risk Reduction Techniques** suggests alternative ways to prevent or reduce losses in the process of providing service.

Risk Management Guide for Nonprofits, Bradley Johnson, United Way of America (1987).

Discusses risk management, indemnification, evaluation, and avoiding risk. This book also provides information on risk financing, purchasing insurance, and workers' compensation (276 pp).

Risk Management: Strategies for Managing Volunteer Programs, Sarah Henson and Bruce Larson, Macduff/Blunt Associates (1988).

Outlines particular risks, discusses policies, procedures, legal agreements and contracts, bylaws, tax status, and records with regard to volunteer programs (132 pp).

Screening Volunteers to Prevent Child Sexual Abuse: A Community Guide for Youth Organizations, National Assembly of National Voluntary Health and Social Welfare Organizations.

How to conduct background checks, summary of Federal laws (32 pp).

Suggested Guidelines for Establishing Volunteer Transportation Programs, Minnesota Governor's Office of Volunteer Services (1978).

Covers planning, the application process for volunteers, driver training, record keeping, volunteer recognition, insurance, and program evaluation. This guidebook is to be used with the agency's or organization's definition of the kind of service it will provide and who is eligible to receive the service (20 pp).

Volunteer Energy Series: Children as Volunteers, Revised, Susan J. Ellis, Katherine H. Noyes, Trina Tracey, and Lawrence Wallace, Energize Associates (1991).

Offers guidelines on how to adopt volunteer management principles for working with children as volunteers. This book also discusses planning and implementing programs, independent projects, legalities, and liabilities (68 pp).

Volunteers and the Law in Maryland, Governor's Office on Volunteerism and the Bar Association of Baltimore City (1989).

Examines some of the issues that arise over volunteer rights and responsibilities. Designed for volunteers and volunteer agencies, it provides a set of simple legal foundations for volunteers (25 pp).

Volunteers and the Law: Legal Rights and Obligations of the Volunteers and Volunteer Agencies, Georgia Office of Volunteer Services (n.d.).

Discusses questions of law as they apply to the rights and responsibilities of volunteers and volunteer agencies (23 pp).

What If Something Happens? A Guide to Risk Management and Insurance Options for Community Service Programs, Crestienne Van Keuien, U.S. Department of Justice, National Institute of Corrections (1988).

Addresses questions about potential liability in programs involving offenders in community service as a means of restitution. This publication provides specific examples of risk management techniques used by agencies administering community service programs in

Newsletters

Legal-Ease, c/o the Center for Nonprofit Management, University of St. Thomas, 1000 LaSalle Avenue, Minneapolis, MN 55403.

A new quarterly newsletter for nonprofit managers and boards. This publication covers questions in the area of nonprofit law.

The Nonprofit Counsel, Wiley Law Publications, P.O. Box 39300, Colorado Springs, CO 80949-9904.

A monthly newsletter on legal and tax issues for nonprofit organizations. Gives up-to-date information on a variety of issues related to nonprofit law, including pending legislation.

Community Resource Organizations

After 10 years of consideration by Congress, the Volunteer Protection Act of 1997 (VPA) was passed and went into effect mid September, 1997. While the purpose of the act is to address the fear of lawsuits against volunteers, the result has been to raise more questions than it answers. The VPA was written so that it would preempt any state law, unless state law provided additional protection. As of the printing of this book, there has been no analysis of how the VPA will fit with the provisions of Minnesota law. The VPA does allow for the state legislature to opt out of the federal law, but that would only apply if all the parties are citizens of the state. If they are from different states, then the federal law applies. Hopefully some action will be taken in the 1999 legislative session to address these issues.

Attorney Generals Office
Charities Division
1200 NCL Tower
445 Minnesota Street
St. Paul, MN 55101 (612) 297-4613
World Wide Web Site: http//www.ag.state.mn.us

Center for Nonprofit Management
Independent Sector
1828 L Street NW
Washington, DC 20036
(202) 223-8100
World Wide Web Site: http//www.indepsec.org

Equal Employment Opportunity Commission (federal)
Minneapolis Area Office
330 2nd Street South Suite 108
Minneapolis, MN 55401-2144
(612) 335-4040

Equal Employment Opportunity Commission (Minneapolis)
Department of Civil Rights
City Hall Suite 239
350 South 5th Street
Minneapolis, MN 55415
(612) 673-3012

Equal Employment Opportunity Commission (state of Minnesota)
Minnesota Department of Human Rights
190 East 5th
St. Paul, MN 55101
(612) 296-5663

Equal Employment Opportunity Commission (St. Paul)
Human Rights Department
515 City Hall
15 Kellogg Boulevard
St. Paul, MN 55102
(612) 298-4288

Management Assistance Program for Nonprofits
2233 University Avenue West, Suite 360
St. Paul, MN 55114
(612) 647-1216
World Wide Web Site: http//www.mapnp.org

Minnesota Council on Nonprofits
2700 University Avenue West, Suite 250
St. Paul, MN 55114
(612) 642-1904
World Wide Web Site: http//www.mncn.org

Minnesota Department of Human Rights
500 Bremer Tower 7th Place and Minnesota Street
St. Paul, MN 55101
(612) 296-5663

Minnesota Department of Human Services
Community and Human Resource Development
444 Lafayette Road, 2nd Floor
St. Paul, MN 55155-3821
(612) 297-7077
World Wide Web Site: http//www.dhs.state.mn.us

Minnesota Insurance information Center
750 Norwest Center
55 Fifth Street East
St. Paul, MN 55101-1764
(612)222-3800 or 1-800-642-6121

Minnesota Office of Citizenship and Volunteer Services
Department of Administration
117 University Avenue
St. Paul, MN 55155
(612)296-4731 or 1-800-652-9747 (greater Minnesota only)
World Wide Web Site: http//www.admin.state.mn.us/mocvs

Minnesota State Bar Association
Minnesota Bar Center
514 Nicollet Mall, Suite 300
Minneapolis, MN 55402
(612) 333-1183
World Wide Web Site: http//www.mnbar.org

Nonprofit Risk Management Center
1001 Connecticut Avenue NW, Suite 900
Washington, DC 20036
(202)785-3891
World Wide Web Site: http//www.nonprofitrisk.org

Public Risk Management Association
Suite 1020
1815 North Fort Myer Drive
Arlington, VA 22209
(703)528-7701
World Wide Web Site: http//www.primacentral.org

Risk Insurance Management Society (RIMS)
655 Third Avenue
New York, NY 10017
(212) 286-9292
World Wide Web Site: http//www.rims.org

The Society of Certified Risk Managers, Technicians & Educational Specialists (SOCRATES)
207 West Maple Avenue
Shiremanstown, PA 17011
World Wide Web Site: http//www.connectyou.com/ins/riskm.html

Note: The Minnesota Department of Human Services offers training on holistic screening of volunteers for sexual abuse. Contact the department at 444 Lafayette Road, St. Paul, MN 55155-3821, (612) 297-7077, or (612) 2974275.

ENDNOTES

1/   Geiger v. Simpson Methodist Episcopal Church, 219 N.W. 463 (Minn. 1928).

2/   Misset v. Cardinal Cushing High School, 680 N.E.2d 563 (Mass. App. 1997).

3/   Mortenson v. Hindahl, 77 N.W.2d 185 (Minn. 1956).

4/   Dellwo v. Pearson, 107 N.W.2d 859 (Minn. 1961).

5/   Johnson v. St. Paul City Ry. Co., 69 N.W. 900 (Minn. 1897).

6/   Bowen v. Arnold, 380 N.W.2d 531 (Minn. App. 1986).

7/   Petron v. Waldo, 139 N.W.2d 484 (Minn. 1965).

8/   Minn. Stat., Section 604A.01(1).

9/   Augustine v. Hitzman, 178 N.W.2d 227 (Minn. 1970).

10/   Ponticas v. K.M.S., 331 N.W.2d 907 (Minn. 1983).

11/   Yunker v. Honeywell, Inc., 496 N.W.2d 419 (Minn. App. 1993).

12/   M.L. v. Magnuson, 531 N.W.2d 849 (Minn. App. 1995).

13/   Minn. Stat., Section 626.556 (relating to minors); Minn. Stat. Section 626.557 (relating to vulnerable adults).

14/   Minn. Stat., Section 626.556(3).

15/   Minn. Stat., Section 626.5572(16).

16/   Big Brother/Big Sister of Metro Atlanta, Inc. v. Terrell, 359 S.E.2d 241 (Ga. App. 1987).

17/   Minn. Stat. ch. 245A.

18/   Richie v. Paramount Pictures Corp., 544 N.W.2d 21 (Minn. 1996).

19/   Lake v. Wal-Mart Stores, Inc., --- N.W.2d ---, 1997 WL 434212 (Minn. App. Aug. 5, 1997).

20/   Stubbs v. North Memorial Medical Center, 448 N.W.2d 78, 82 (Minn. App. 1989).

21/   Minn. Stat., Section 317A.241(6).

22/   Minn. Stat., Section 317A.251.

23/   Minn. Stat., Section 317A.257.

24/   Rehn v. Fischley, 557 N.W.2d 328 (Minn. 1997).

25/   Minn. Stat., Section 317A.255.

26/   Ray v. Homewood Hospital, 27 N.W.2d 409 (Minn. 1947).

27/   Bunia v. Knight Ridder, 544 N.W.2d 60 (Minn. App. 1996).

28/   Schlobohm v. Spa Petite, Inc., 326 N.W.2d 920 (Minn. 1982).

29/   Schlobohm v. Spa Petite, Inc., 326 N.W.2d 920 (Minn. 1982).

30/   Nimis v. St. Paul Turners, 521 N.W.2d 54 (Minn. App. 1994).

31/   Malecha v. St. Croix Valley Skydiving Club, Inc., 392 N.W.2d 727 (Minn. App. 1986).

32/   Malecha v. St. Croix Valley Skydiving Club, Inc., 392 N.W.2d 727 (Minn. App. 1986) (citing Larsen v. Vic Tanny International, 474 N.E.2d 729 (Ill. App. 1984)).

33/   Minn. Stat., Section 604.02.

34/   Minn. Stat., Section 3.732.

35/   Minn. Stat., Section 3.732.

36/   Minn. Stat., Section 3.739.

37/   Minn. Stat. ch. 466.

38/   Minn. Stat., Section 466.01.

39/   Minn. Stat., Section 317A.257.

40/   Minn. Stat., Section 604A.11.

41/   Minn. Stat., Section 604A.10.

42/   Minn. Stat., Section 604A.12.

43/   Minn. Stat., Section 604A.01(1).

44/   Minn. Stat., Section 317A.521

Glossary

Accounts receivable insurance - protects against inability to collect accounts receivable due to loss of supporting records.

Actual cash value - in property insurance, settling a loss based on replacement cost at the time of loss, less depreciation.

Adjuster - a person who determines the amount of loss. Company or independent adjusters represent the insurer. Public adjusters represent the policyholder.

Agent - a person who has authority to act for another. In insurance, agents sell directly to the policyholder. By contract and bylaw, the agent is endowed with many powers of the insurer.

All risk policy and property insurance - covers loss by any peril not specifically excluded. (Valuable paper insurance covers all risks.) In contrast, a named peril policy covers only certain listed perils. (Insurance on buildings is often limited to loss from fire, wind, hail, vandalism, and other specified perils.)

Amount of insurance - the limit that an insurer will pay under a policy.

Annual statement- summary of an insurer's operation for the year and balance sheet with exhibits. Filed with each state in which the insurer is licensed to sell insurance.

Application - a written statement by prospective policyholder. The insurer relies on this statement when issuing the insurance. (An application for automobile insurance may ask for information on previous accidents and losses. If the applicant reports no previous accidents or losses, the insurer agrees to issue the policy and give a rate credit for no accidents.)

Assume - to undertake a risk when agreeing to offer insurance. Nonprofits may decline to buy insurance and thus assume (retain) a risk.

Audit - to review policyholder records to verify the accuracy of premiums paid. Certain insurance policies give the insurer the privilege of performing this review. (In workers compensation insurance, a deposit premium is paid on the basis of the expected premium for the following year. At the end of the year, the insurer requests records of actual payroll to determine the actual premium payable.)

Automobile liability insurance - protects against legal liability for bodily injury and property damage arising from ownership or operation of automobiles.

Bailment - delivery of personal property to another to be held and returned to the owner, in good condition.

Blanket crime policy - a broad policy providing coverage for employee dishonesty, money and securities (on or off premises), counterfeit currency, and depositors forgery protection. One amount of insurance applies to all coverages.

Blanket position bond - insures an employer against loss by dishonest acts of employees. (See also Commercial blanket bond and Fidelity bond.)

Book value - value of assets (bonds, stocks, real and personal property) as shown in a policyholder's books of account.

Broker - a legal representative of the policyholder. The broker negotiates with insurers for the policyholder and usually receives commission from the insurer.

Burglary - theft involving illegal entry (break-in).

Business Interruption coverages - form of insurance that protects against lost income when a policyholder's buildings or personal property are damaged.

Cargo - goods being transported by land, air, or water.

Catastrophe - a severe loss, usually affecting many policyholders. Examples are earthquake, tornado, or widespread fire.

Certificate of insurance - document issued by an insurer, insurance agent, or broker. This document is issued as evidence to third party that the policyholder maintains certain coverage, usually automobile or general liability insurance.

Civil liability - liability from actions due to negligence, breach of contract, or any wrong other than criminal actions.

Claim - the amount which the policyholder believes an insurer should pay for a covered loss. When this amount is established, the claim becomes a loss. In practice, the words claim and loss are used synonymously.

Claims-made Insurance - liability insurance that covers claims against the policyholder that are made during the policy period, regardless of when the accident occurred. In contrast, an occurrence policy covers accidents that took place during the policy period even if the event is not discovered until after the policy period.

Collision - the result of an automobile striking an object or another vehicle. Collision insurance covers this loss.

Commercial blanket bond - insures an employer against loss from dishonest acts committed by employees. (Also see Blanket position bond and Fidelity bond.)

Commercial multiple peril - a package policy that includes both property and liability insurance.

Commission - the portion of the premium allowed to the agent or broker.

Commissioner of insurance - state official who enforces insurance laws and directs state insurance departments. In Minnesota, the commissioner of commerce has this duty.

Completed operations - the liability a contractor might incur after the job has been completed. This liability results from improperly performed work.

Comprehensive general liability - a policy providing broad coverage for claims of bodily injury and property damage. The policy covers acts of policyholders and acts of others for whom the policyholder may be liable.

Compulsory insurance - insurance required by a state or other governmental unit, including workers compensation and automobile liability. Some states may require other forms of liability insurance.

Concealment - the failure to disclose a material fact. (Material facts are those the insurer considers essential in deciding whether to offer coverage.) This failure may void an insurance policy.

Consequential loss - an indirect loss caused by an insured peril. An example is loss of income caused by damage or destruction of a building or personal property.

Contingent business Interruption loss due to the interruption of business, by fire or other perils, at the premises of a supplier, customer, or utility service.

Contingent liability - liability incurred by the policyholder for damages arising out of the acts or omissions of others (such as independent contractors). This does not include employees or agents.

Contract - every kind of oral or written agreement that has legal consequences for the parties involved. A promise that creates or modifies a legal relationship between parties.

Contractual liability - liability set forth by agreement. This is distinguished from liability imposed by law (legal liability).

Court bonds - bonds often required to be filed before one can take legal action in the courts.

Covenant - a written agreement (contract) signed and notarized between two or more people, in which one party or parties promises to perform certain acts (or refrain from certain acts) and the other party or parties agree to give compensation for such performance.

Coverage - the extent of protection offered by an insurance policy.

CPCU (Chartered Property and Casualty Underwriter) - a professional designation conferred by the American Institute for Property and Liability Underwriters.

Criminal liability - liability imposed by governmental laws, rules, and regulations.

Damages - the amount of money awarded to compensate for a loss by injury to a person, that person's property, or by rights established by law.

Data processing insurance - covers physical loss or damage to computer equipment, data, media, and the extra expense of continuing operations after loss or damage. It also offers business interruption coverage if the damage causes a shutdown of operations.

Deductible - the amount of a loss to be retained (paid) by the policyholder.

Depositors forgery bond - insures the organization against loss from forgery or alteration of checks and drafts issued by that organization.

Depreciation - reduction in the value of tangible property caused by physical deterioration or obsolescence.

Direct writer - an insurer that sells insurance through employees licensed as agents, or through independent agents who represent only that insurer.

Directors and owners liability Insurance - protects officers and directors against claims of alleged negligence or wrongful acts in the course of their duties. Also covers the corporation for expenses of defending lawsuits arising from alleged negligence or wrongful acts of directors and officers.

Disability - inability to carry on one's normal work duties due to injury or illness.

Disclosure - a statement revealing the risks and responsibilities associated with a certain activity or situation.

Discrimination - practices which exclude or promote bias against a certain person or groups of people.

Employer's liability Insurance - covers common law liability of an employer for employee injuries. This is distinguished from liability imposed by workers compensation laws.

Endorsement - an addition to a policy that clarifies or changes coverage. Also called a rider.

Errors and omissions Insurance - covers mistakes made in providing a service (insurance, real estate, public accounting, etc.). It is similar to professional liability insurance.

Exclusion - a loss that is not covered, as stated in an insurance policy.

Extra expense Insurance - reimburses a policyholder for extra expenses of continuing business following loss or damage to property.

Feasance - the performance of an act.

Fidelity bond - covers an employer's loss due to employee dishonesty or embezzlement. (See also Blanket crime policy, Blanket position bond, and Commercial blanket bonds.)

Fiduciary - a person who occupies a position of trust, especially one who manages the affairs of another.

Fiduciary relations - relationship of an informal nature in which one person trusts fully and relies upon another. Directors or corporations serve in a fiduciary capacity when performing duties for the benefit of clients or others.

Financial guaranty - a guarantee that another person or entity will pay a sum of money. This is one type of surety bond.

Governmental Immunity - most states and the federal government have statutes relating to tort claims against governmental entities. These statutes state that the entities cannot be held liable for certain claims.

Hold-harmless agreement - an obligation assumed by contract to pay damages for which another is legally liable. Liability of one party is assumed by a second party.

Improvements and betterments - additions made to buildings by the tenant. The tenant has an insurable interest in these additions for the term of the lease.

Indemnification - the act of restoring the victim of a loss, in whole or part, by payment, repair, or replacement. Insurance is a form of indemnity; however, it can be more than this. Therefore insurance and indemnification are not the same.

Indemnity - making good another's losses. Compensation for loss, damage, or injury; reimbursement. Indemnity is the obligation of one person to make good any loss or damage another person has incurred or may incur.

Insurance - type of contract between two parties: One party, in return for regular payments of certain sums of money by the other, promises to pay for specified losses, liabilities, or damages incurred by the second party while the contract is in effect.

Insurance Guaranty Act - state legislation that collects money from insurance companies to reimburse policyholders and claimants of insolvent insurers. (Sometimes called an Insurance Insolvency Act.) Minnesota has such a law.

Insured - a person or organization protected by an insurance policy and entitled to recover for loss under its terms.

Insurer - an insurance company.

Intentional tort - any deliberate invasion of personal or property rights.

Joint tort - a wrong to be shared by two or more people.

Legal liability - liability imposed by law, as opposed to liability arising from a contract. An example of legal liability is that arising from an automobile accident.

Lessee - a tenant who has signed a lease.

Lessor - an owner of property who rents it to another under a lease contract.

Liability - a legal duty, obligation, or debt. A legal term that includes almost every aspect of responsibility.

Liability insurance - insures policyholders for damages they maybe obligated to pay others as the result of negligence.

Liable - having a duty or obligation to another person that is enforceable in court.

Libel - to publish defamatory statements about another.

Loss prevention - inspection or engineering work on insured risks that helps remove potential causes of loss. This is a function of insurers, agents, or brokers.

Malpractice - improper professional actions, or failure to exercise proper professional skills. This term applies to professional advisers such as physicians, dentists, and lawyers.

Material fact - a fact, which if known by an insurer, would have influenced it not to write a policy on the terms on which it was written-or not to write the policy at all.

Medical payments insurance - pays the cost of medical care to an injured person, regardless of policyholder liability for the injury. Written in conjunction with general liability and automobile insurance.

Misfeasance - the improper doing of an act; negligence.

Money and securities Insurance covers loss or destruction of money and securities from almost any cause except employee dishonesty and forgery. This insurance applies inside and outside the insured premises.

Mysterious disappearance - unexplained loss of insured property.

Named insured - a person or organization named in and protected by a policy, as opposed to someone who may have an interest in the policy but is not named.

Negligence - the absence of care expected of a reasonably prudent person. Conduct that falls below the standard set by law for protecting others against risk or harm. An unintentional tort characterized by inadvertence, thoughtlessness, or inattention. Negligence may result from doing something or failing to do something.

Non-admitted - an insurance company not licensed by the state.

No-fault automobile Insurance - coverage designed to meet the needs of a legal system that compensates victims of automobile accidents without proof of negligence on anyone's part. No-fault laws provide that a victim's own insurance will provide reimbursement for medical and funeral expenses and lost income, within specified limits. Once expenses or injuries surpass the stipulated threshold (monetary or otherwise), the victim may sue. Minnesota has a no-fault law.

Nonfeasance - the failure to perform a required duty; negligence.

Non-ownership automobile liability coverage - insurance against liability incurred while using an automobile not owned or hired by the policyholder.

Occupational disease - impairment of health due to continuous exposure to hazards inherent in person's job. This loss is compensated under most state workers compensation laws.

Occupational Safety and Health Act of 1970 (OSHA) - a federal law establishing safe and healthy working conditions. The act sets job safety and health standards enforced by Labor Department inspectors. It also requires employers to report work injuries and illnesses and keep records of these incidents. Various states, including Minnesota, have OSHA laws stricter than the federal law.

Package policy - see Commercial multiple peril.

Peril - the cause of loss; a fire, explosion, accident, etc.

Personal injury protection - extensions of a liability policy, covering losses other than bodily injury. These extensions include false arrest, libel, slander, and invasion of privacy. The term personal injury in its broadest sense includes sexual harassment and similar offenses, although some personal injury offenses are uninsurable.

Personal property - property other than buildings and real estate (office equipment, supplies, etc.)

Plaintiff - the party who claims to be injured and brings a suit for recovery of damages (tort).

Policy - a definite course of action, selected from among alternatives and in light of given conditions, to guide decisions.

Policyholder - the party paying a premium to an insurer in return for the insurer's promise to provide protection under the insurance policy.

Principal - in surety bonds, the principal is one whose ability to perform is guaranteed by the bond.

Protective liability Insurance - protects against liability arising from a secondary cause, such as an act of a contractor.

Punitive damages - damages awarded separately and in addition to compensatory damages, usually as a result of malicious or wanton misconduct. These damages are meant to punish the wrongdoer and deter others from similar misconduct. Some forms of liability insurance exclude coverage for punitive damages.

Replacement cost - the cost to replace damaged or destroyed property without deduction for depreciation. See Actual cash value.

Release - a contract by which a person, the releasor, agrees to give up a claim or right to someone against whom it could be legally enforced. A general release covers all claims between the parties that exist or are contemplated at the time the release is executed. A specific release is confined to particular claims that are specified in it.

Representation - information given to an insurer by the policyholder which may influence insurer's agreement to write the insurance, or the amount of premium charged.

Risk - the chance of loss. Risk provides the reason that people buy insurance.

Risk and Insurance Management Society (RIMS) - an association formed in 1950 to foster the profession of risk management. It acts as a nonprofit clearinghouse for information on risk management and sound insurance procurement practices. RIMS carries out research and sponsors local and national education programs. RIMS has a Minnesota Chapter in the Minneapolis-St. Paul area.

Risk assumption - keeping the risk and accepting the responsibility for any losses that may occur.

Risk avoidance - eliminating risk by eliminating the risky situation or activity.

Risk reduction - implementing policies and procedures to lessen risk exposure.

Risk transfer - transferring the risk to someone else via insurance, leases, contracts, or other agreements.

Self insurance - term mistakenly used in describing an entity that decides to retain its own risk. The retention may be funded (with a reserve) or unfunded (paid as an expense). Self "insurance" is technically not insurance, because there is no transfer of risk or pooling of risk.

Statute of limitations - specification of the time within which you may start certain types of lawsuits.

Surety bond - an agreement providing monetary compensation for failure to perform specified acts within a stated time. These agreements include license bonds, construction bonds, and bail bonds.

Tort - A private, or civil, wrong or injury other than breach of contract or governmental law. A civil (as opposed to criminal) wrong, other than a breach of contract, done to another person. The law of torts deals with the allocation of responsibility for loss or harm arising out of human activities. The court will provide remedies for torts in the form of action for damages.

Training - instruction that is provided in order to improve performance on the job.

Umbrella liability insurance - protects a policyholder for claims in excess of primary automobile, general liability, and employers liability insurance limits. This insurance also covers some claims excluded by these primary insurance policies, subject to a $10,000 or higher deductible.

Vicarious liability - the liability that is imposed on the organization for the acts of employees and volunteers acting on the behalf of the organization and with the organization's authorization.

Voluntary compensation coverage - insurance that offers volunteers a coverage similar to workers compensation insurance. Organizations may offer this coverage in Minnesota.

Waiver - giving up or surrendering of a right or privilege that is known to exist. In insurance, this may be a provision or rider agreeing to forego a premium payment or to exclude liability for a stated cause of accident.

Note: Portions of this glossary were reprinted with permission from *Risk Management: Strategiies fro Managing Volunteer Programs by* Sarah Henson and Bruce Larson, Macduff/Bunt Associates, Inc. 1998.

Index

Notes